CHRISTIAN MATURITY:

A Spirituality for Adult Catholics

by

Pierre-André Liégé, O.P.

Original Translation and Introduction
by
Thomas C. Donlan, O.P.
Dominican Province of St. Albert the Great

Edited with a New Introduction
by
Charles E. Bouchard, O.P.
Dominican Province of St. Albert the Great

NEW PRIORY PRESS
EXPLORING THE DOMINICAN VISION

Chicago 2014

PIERRE-ANDRE LIEGE, O.P.

This book is a translation of *Adultes dans le Christ*, by Pierre-André Liégé, O.P., published by *La Pensée Catholique* (Brussels, Belgium, 1958.) It has been translated into Dutch, German, Catalan, Castilian, Portugese, and Italian.

Original English Edition, 1965
Revisores Ordinis: Augustine Rock, O.P.; Bernard O'Riley, O.P.
Imprimi potest: Gilbert J. Graham, O.P., Provincial.
Nihil obstat: Bernard O'Riley, O.P., Censor Deputatus.

Imprimatur:
+ Most Rev. Cletus F. O'Donnell, J.C.D.,
Administrator, Archdiocese of Chicago, August 16, 1965.

The *Nihil obstat* and *Imprimatur* are official declarations that a book or pamphlet is free of doctrinal or moral error. No implication is contained therein that those who have granted the *Nihil obstat* and *Imprimatur* agree with the contents, opinions, or statements expressed.

Library of Congress Catalogue Number 65-28348
© Copyright 1965 by The Priory Press
2005 South Ashland Avenue, Chicago, Illinois 60608
Manufactured in the United States of America

Revised Edition, 2014.
Copyright by New Priory Press,
1910 S. Ashland Avenue, Chicago, Illinois 60608
This revised English edition is published with the permission of
P. Lachenaud, O.P., Provincial, Province of France.
September, 2014.
Production Editor: Albert Judy, O.P.
Cover Design: Susan Webb.

Contents

Introduction to the Second English Edition v
  Is Maturity an Issue Today? viii
  Christian Maturity and Discipleship viii
  Christian Maturity and Virtue x
  The Unity of Personality xi

Introduction to the 1965 English Edition xiv

I Human Maturity and Christian Maturity 23
  What Is Human Maturity? 25
  Outline of the Solution to the Problem 28
  Approach to a Twofold Maturity 30

II Achieving Maturity of Faith 33
  The Adult Believer Must Be a Convert 35
  God in the Faith of an Adult 39
  The Unity of Mature Faith 43

III Achieving Mature Charity 49
  The Maturity of Charity and the Motives Proposed by the Gospels 50
  The Maturity of Charity and the Unity of the Personality 51
  The Maturity of Charity in the Social Dimension 53
  The Maturity of Charity and the Acceptance of Realities 55

IV Growing Spiritually in the Church 59
Integration into Social Life and Awareness of the Church..................60
The Church is an Eschatological Community..60
The Church as the Institution of Salvation...62
Motives for Living in the Church..64
Toward a More Catholic Appreciation of the Church..........................65
Life in the Real Church...66

V Christian Maturity and Obedience.. 69
The Sources of Christian Obedience..71
The Mature Exercise of Christian Obedience..74

VI The Spirit of Penance in the Mature Christian........................... 79
The Metanoia of the Gospels and Penance...80
Penance in the Gospel and the Mature Sense of Sin............................86
The Adult Christian and the Sacrament of Penance.............................90
Practices of Penance and the Penitential Life of the Adult................94
Preparing Adults for the Self-denial of the Gospels............................. 99

Scriptural Index...99

Introduction to the Second English Edition

My inspiration for this new edition came from Fr. Paul Philibert, who with Fr. Thomas O'Meara described the groundbreaking work of Fr. Liégé in their book *Scanning the Signs of the Time: French Dominicans in the Twentieth Century*. In it, they describe his contribution to the renewal of catechetics, his understanding of the Church as a mystery of the sacramental life and holiness, rather than merely as an institution, and his efforts to turn kerygmatic theology (itself a new and unfamiliar idea) into an adult approach to Christian life. It is worthwhile noting that he also served as the first homiletics professor at the Saulchoir, and helped put the "P" back in "O.P." Like other mid-20th centry French Dominicans, he was a true innovator who went back to the sources in order to renew the Church and the Order.

One of St. Thomas Aquinas' most famous teachings is *"gratia perficit naturam"* – grace perfects nature. This is the root of the Catholic understanding of the human person. The meaning of this phrase is not obvious unless we consider its alternative, "grace destroys nature (in order to replace it)." This has never been explicitly articulated as Christian doctrine, but it is often an unspoken assumption that leads to disaster in the spiritual life.

It is the basis of various forms of false asceticism which demean and degrade the human body; it was the foundation of Manicheanism in the 4th century, which St. Augustine fought against; and it was the later basis of numerous medieval heresies, such as Albigensianism (which St. Dominic preached against). Each of these are based on the basic unacceptability of human nature, its incompatibility with grace.

The doctrine of the Incarnation belies this. If this dualistic view of human nature were true, God could not have assumed human nature and become human. The fact that Jesus was both fully human and fully God is proof that human nature, even though wounded by sin, is "good enough" to bear the weight of grace, good enough to be saved without being destroyed. By extension, incarnational theology tells us that human persons, all of creation in fact, are "good enough" to mediate grace, or even "cause" grace in a certain sense. This is the basis of our sacramental system in which ordinary things like bread, water, wine, oil, spoken words – can be the occasion of grace in real, tangible lives. Grace and created things, in the Catholic view, are not opposed or antithetical, but relatively compatible. This is also a fundamental difference between Catholic and Protestant theology. Even though the Reformers were right that grace is fully unmerited and other, they often did not allow that it could find a true home in human existence. Our belief in the relative compatibility of nature and grace makes it possible for us to speak of virtue; for us virtue is a merger or integration of human effort with grace such that we acquire "graced habits" that perdure within us. Grace is not a flash in the pan, a sudden and frightening intervention of God, but rather a stream of energy that empowers and delights us.

Of course, grace is not always delightful. Sometimes it is downright painful. As C. E. Morgan says, describing the fiction of Flannery O'Connor: "In story after story we see characters broken open by the hard fist of the writer, acts of brutality O'Connor deemed necessary for the eruption of living grace into the stubborn, recalcitrant lives of both the nonbelieving and the self-professedly devout. In O'Connor's fiction, the worldly trappings of the individual must be removed by force, not because her God is an angry God, but because most of us – when the ugly truth is told – would prefer to go to the grave with our vices intact, damnation be damned." Surely Fr. Liégé, who speaks of the "hard reality of charity" and warns against "sugar and spice" Christianity, would appreciate this side of grace. But even when grace hurts, or perhaps especially when it hurts, it is part of the transition into adult faith.

This basic insight is the foundation of Fr. Liégé's book, *Adults in Christ*. In it, he takes the thought of Aquinas as well as the

Scriptural witness and introduces them to the field of psychology which was becoming the cultural *lingua franca* in the 1950s when he wrote. He restates the basic question over and over again: Can one be spiritually mature without being humanly mature? His answer is no, at least not without a miracle. Grace respects human growth and the integrity of human life, so it only finds a comfortable home when the human personality is adequately mature to integrate it. Stories of child saints are quaint but suspicious. God prefers to make grace proportionate to our ability to receive it. God could overwhelm the human person with miraculous interventions of grace, but chooses not to do so. God created good things that are radically open to their ultimate purpose or destiny. St. Thomas, like Aristotle before him, notes that creatures have natural purposes. They know how to migrate, how to build nests, how to avoid predators. If God has planted this instinctive knowledge in them, Aquinas reasons, how much more would God plant in rational creatures the knowledge of and desire for their own ultimate purpose? This purpose is eternal life with God. Thomas O'Meara summarizes Aquinas' view beautifully:

> There is only one primary or ultimate cause: that is God. But creatures – inevitably secondary causes – are not puppets. They are real agents, fashioning out of their natures active forms this existence. A star burns, a tanager builds a nest. The power of God is revealed the variety of creatures who are proper causes of their actions. God appears supreme not by miraculously replacing them with unnatural displays of power but by endowing them with their own modes of activity. God gives independence to creatures not by a lack of power, but by an immensity of goodness; he wishes to communicate to things a resemblance to him in that they would not only exist but be the cause of others...[1]

---

[1] *Thomas Aquinas Theologian* (Notre Dame: University of Notre Dame Press, 1999) 76.

Is Maturity an Issue Today?

In the original introduction to the English edition, Fr. Donlan asserts that maturity was an issue in the 1950s when Fr. Liégé wrote, and in the 1960s, when Fr. Donlan produced the English translation. What about today, early into the 21st century?

It appears from a quick internet search that there is a significant body of material on the problem of maturity in young adults.[2] In his book *Artificial Maturity*, Tim Elmore says that for a number of reasons, "students are stunted in their emotional maturity. ...Students are consuming information they aren't completely ready to handle. The adult part of their brain is still forming and isn't ready to apply all that our society throws at it. Their mind takes it in and files it, but their will and emotions are not prepared to act on it in a healthy way." Elmore goes on to list "marks of maturity" that echo many of the themes found in Liégé's book.

Christian Maturity and Discipleship

In her groundbreaking work *Forming Intentional Disciples*, Sherry Weddell has identified the Achilles' heel of contemporary Catholicism. She notes that despite solid participation by Catholics in their Churches (even allowing for reduced Church attendance and participation in the sacraments), Catholics have largely failed to embrace a personal relationship with Christ that is a sign of authentic Christian maturity. She would say that

---

[2] See for example, Terri Apter, *The Myth of Maturity: What Teenagers Need from Parents to Become Adults"* (Terri Apter); or Tim Elmore, *Artificial Maturity: Helping Kids Meet the Challenge of Becoming Authentic Adults* (Norcross, Georgia: Growing Leaders, 2012). Seminal work on the topic of moral maturity was done by Swiss psychiatrist Jean Piaget, a contemporary of and probably a source for Liégé; and Lawrence Kohlberg, who became famous for his six stages of moral development.

although Catholics are sacramentalized, they have not really been evangelized. Many, she says, don't even know that a personal relationship with Christ is possible. I believe that she is correct. The key to revitalizing our parishes – and the Church in general – is showing Catholics that deep conversion and a personal relationship with Christ are not only possible, but necessary to the life of faith. They are not as she says, "optional accessories" only for the spiritual elite. They are a basic goal for anyone who says "I believe."

She describes three spiritual journeys that we go through in the spiritual life: the personal, the ecclesial, and the journey of active practice (54). She also describes five "thresholds" in the journey toward discipleship. These are initial trust, spiritual curiosity, spiritual openness, spiritual seeking, and finally, intentional discipleship. These clearly suggest stages in spiritual maturity, culminating in an adult relationship with Christ (125ff). The problem is that each of these thresholds can be frightening, and many of us, even priests, fail to step across them because we lack the maturity to do so. We remain in our comfort zone, not even aware of what is on the other side.

This final stage of discipleship, when accompanied by adult maturity, is the flowering of a vocation. A vocation is not something that is thrust upon us, but something offered by God, and accepted. Weddell describes a vocation not as an ecclesial career, but as a "supernatural mystery that emerges from a sustained encounter with Christ. It is a transforming, sanctifying path and work of love to which Christ calls us. A vocation builds on natural qualities but carries us far beyond what we would imagine" (89). Children do not have sustained personal encounters with Christ, adults do. I believe that Fr. Liégé would agree with her theory about discipleship and I believe he would say that it can only emerge in a person who has achieved a certain level of "natural" maturity. Unfortunately, we have allowed ourselves to be carried along on a superficial wave of ecclesial belonging which does not automatically translate into discipleship.

Christian Maturity and Virtue

Many Catholics have apparently rejected their religion in favor of Evangelical Christianity or a non-religious "spirituality" because they don't see the point of religious rules and laws that guide organized religion. Some of these rules *are* pointless, and it is hard to connect them to any deep doctrinal truths. Many others, especially rules relating to traditional religious disciplines like fasting, confession, sexual abstinence, almsgiving and regular participation in the Eucharist and other sacraments, are the mature expression of one's faith. Once we understand that mature faith requires formation or training, we are willing to commit to regular involvement. This is analogous to the realization that physical fitness requires a regular routine of strenuous and sometimes boring exercises that keep us in shape. This is not to say that religious observance needs to be boring, but rather that it becomes more meaningful to us once we see the ultimate purpose of it.

The virtues are incarnations of grace. They are a sign that God means what he says – that he saves us. This salvation is body and soul. So virtues are real human habits, or skills that prepare us achieve the holiness that God calls us to. When we achieve some measure of justice, or prudence or humility or courage, we resemble God's self and we come closer to being citizens of God's kingdom.

The Catholic understanding of virtue is undergirded by a profound theology of grace as compatible with human nature (and maturity); but it is complex and difficult to catechize. It is the difference between "do this because I said so," and "do this because it is deeply satisfying and a perfection of your natural destiny by grace." For this reason, the Church at times took the easy way and opted for a relatively legalistic and obedience-based understanding of faith and the moral life.³ This works well for children, but it is not adequate for an adult understanding of the moral and spiritual life. Virtues are habits, qualities of personality that reflect a merging of human ability and grace. Rowan Williams, former Archbishop of Canterbury, describes a similar dynamic as he talks about prayer:

> Growing in prayer is not simply acquiring a set of spiritual skills that operate in one bit of your life. It is about growing into what St. Paul calls "the measure of the full stature of Christ" (Eph 4:13). It is growing into the kind of humanity that Christ shows us. Growing in prayer, in other words, is growing in Christian humanity.⁴

These virtues are acquired only with intentional effort. They are not just discrete and unrelated skills but part who we are. Once acquired they are relatively durable and begin to shape future choices and actions, and open us to grace.

The Unity of Personality

Liégé refers many times to the unity of personality. Another way to describe this is to say that someone is "integrated," or that they "have it together." Many moral failings result from a "disintegrated" personality, one that is at war with itself. This occurs when I believe one thing but do another (Rom 7:15-20), or when I give into desires that I know are wrong, but I can't resist the immediate satisfaction they bring. The truly holy person is of one mind; she desires the one thing and her life is an attempt to bring everything she does into line with that one thing. We look

---

³John Mahoney, S.J. in *The Making of Moral Theology* (New York: Oxford, 1997) describes how this well-intentioned shift had disastrous results for Catholics right up until the 1960s (see especially pp. 22-36). For a more concise summary, see my *Whatever Happened to Sin?* (Chicago, New Priory Press, 2013), especially Chapter 1, "The Changing Shape of Moral Theology").
⁴ Rowan Williams, "In the Place of Jesus: Insights from Origen on Prayer." *Christian Century* (August 6, 2014), 20-22, at 20.

for integration in a prospective employee, friend or spouse. Does this person act predictably? Are her actions consistent with what he says she believes? Conflict between what we really want or value and what we do is perhaps the biggest single source of human pain.

The popular Quaker author and speaker Parker Palmer describes this lack of unity as a basic spiritual problem. In his book *A Hidden Wholeness*, he says that most of us lead a divided life, which he describes as a "personal pathology, and a "failure of human wholeness." He would describe the achievement of wholeness, or personal integrity, as an aspect of human maturity. He says, "living integral lives as adults is far more daunting than recovering our childhood capacity to commute between two worlds. As adults, we must achieve a complex integration that spans the contradictions between inner and outer reality that supports both personal integrity and the common good."[5] He makes it clear that this is hard work and is a lifelong journey, but it is also a journey that all of us who seek holiness must undertake.

I'm sure that Fr. Liégé would agree with him.

Charles E. Bouchard, O.P., S.T.D.
St. Pius Priory
Chicago, Illinois
October 1, 2014

Editor's note on translation: I have retained most of Fr. Donlan's original translation, with a few exceptions to make it more acceptable to the modern ear. I have simplified some cumbersome phrases and I have eliminated references to "man" and "his" in favor of "adults" and "their" or "we" and "our". This

---

[5] *A Hidden Wholeness: The Journey Toward an Undivided Life*. San Francisco, Jossey-Bass, 2005, pp. 6, 7 and 21.

inclusiveness clearly part of the author's original intention.

PIERRE-ANDRE LIEGE, O.P.

Introduction to the 1965 English Edition

The powerful social, political, and economic forces that have shaped the modem world have not been much influenced by Christians or their ideals. While thinkers have recognized this for a long time, it is only recently that the fact is beginning to be realized more popularly. We hear of the Church spoken of as a "diaspora" and as a small remnant among the vast masses of humanity.

The colonial powers of the West are withdrawing from or being driven out of their territorial possessions. New nations are arising from the former colonies. The vast majority of these are outside the sphere of Christian influence. Most of their inhabitants belong to non-Christian religions.

The world was once regarded by many Christians as an obstacle rather than an opportunity. But for over four centuries a splintered Christendom has tended to become more introverted and institutionalized. The desire for spiritual security amidst the nearly incomprehensible changes in the world has had a profound influence upon theology and piety. Individualism has gained the ascendance.

In many parts of a Europe that was once Christian, the peoples' commitment to the faith has weakened dangerously. The working classes were largely lost to the Church after the Industrial Revolution. Externals continue to be maintained in some places where religious vitality is lacking. The Church in Europe is often regarded as a status symbol of the middle class, and it is rejected more because of its disciples than because of its doctrines.

Christians have been accused of not being concerned about and of not being involved in human affairs. The criticism has not always come from neutral or hostile sources. It can be found in the writings of many Church leaders and in papal encyclicals. Yet, the average Christian has not often taken such criticism to heart sufficiently. He has not acted upon it nor has he changed his attitude. He rightly sees danger in involvement. He suffers from the common human affliction of wanting to be safe. He tends to identify prudence with caution rather than with courage. Delay, he thinks, is preferable to the risk of destruction.

The missionary vocation of the Christian is surely not a call to rash action by the ill prepared. It is, rather, a demand for preparation, for facing the realities of both the Church and the world and for developing a genuine Christian spirit and attitude. It is a call to grow up in Christ. It is a demand that Christians should be mature in their faith as they should be mature in every phase of their lives.

The spirit of individualism and the pursuit of spiritual security in an institutionalized Christendom have inevitably produced a regrettable immaturity in many followers of Christ. This is evident today in many ways. The reaction of some Catholics to the workings of the Second Vatican Council is one example. The Church's self-examination shocks many who had identified externals with essentials and discipline with doctrine. At another extreme, the willingness of the Church to enter into ecumenical discussions with fellow Christians and with non-Christians has raised unrealistic hopes for unity among those who are doctrinally naive. Some seem to hope that what they know vaguely as "biblical theology" will bring a profound understanding of faith without the grueling work of hard study. Others appear to believe that greater participation in a more authentic and revitalized liturgy will solve most of the Church's problems.

Yet, all of this is a childish expectation of miracles and an infantile hope that holy water will substitute for sweat. It is a testimonial to immaturity.

It is to offset such unrealistic attitudes and to provide a reliable guide to the acquisition of an authentic, mature spirituality that

Pierre-Andre Liege, O.P.

Père Pierre-André Liégé, O.P., has written this short but profound book. The title of the French original is *Adultes dans le Christ.* Translated literally as *Adults in Christ,* it loses much of its force. For this reason, the title of this English version has been changed to *Consider Christian Maturity.* That is the purpose of the book: to get people to ponder and to understand what produces Christian maturity.

Père Liégé is an excellent teacher, and he begins by analyzing the psychological stages through which a human being must pass if he is to become a responsible adult. These are things we all know by experience, observation, and study. He points out that spiritual growth must parallel the psychological development of the human person. Yet, he is most careful always to indicate that there is, or should be, a parallel between nature and grace and not any causal relationship, as if natural development could bring about spiritual growth. A profound knowledge of the theology of grace is at work here as well as a great insight into human psychology.

Faith is the foundation of the Christian life. Yet, faith is not something static. It must grow by expanding and by deepening. The stages of childhood, adolescence, and adulthood which are discernable in the physical and psychological orders have parallels in the realm of faith. A stunted faith is something monstrous. The man who has attained a mature cultural development, but whose knowledge of the faith remains at the level of the catechism, is incapable of relating his beliefs to his everyday life. Such a man cannot share properly in the missionary vocation of the Christian. He cannot realize his full potential in Christ precisely because he is immature in his faith.

A proper education in the faith is indispensable if Christians are to be realistically engaged in shaping the world according to the ideals of the Gospel. Teaching must present the faith not simply as something to be known, but as something to be embraced. At the very heart of the Christian life is the element of conversion, of a conversion that must be renewed daily and not simply recalled from a distant past and taken for granted. Nor must faith be confused with a vague assent to the existence of God which can be no more than an unspecified religious feeling. Christian faith is explicitly supernatural. It is a work of grace. It focuses upon Jesus Christ. Such an authentic faith provides a kind of spiritual center of gravity for the entire life of an adult. Thus equipped, he becomes free to extend the Kingdom without rashness, without clinging to trivial, pietistic supports, and without the expectation of dramatic and easy success.

The growth in faith must be reflected in a comparable maturity of love. This must surpass mere sentiments of good fellowship, benevolence, or human piety. Christian love must find its motivation in the Gospel; it must be frankly supernatural. It can utilize good natural inclinations, but it must refine and ennoble them by being dedicated to a higher ideal in Christ.

It is in love that the Christian must seek the meaning of his entire life. And such a love must not be allowed to remain childish or sentimentalized. Love must exist at every level of the Christian's life – personal, familial, and social. It must be based on a genuine realization of the needs of others, and not upon any childish, subjective attitude which is basically self-seeking. Only such a mature love will enable the Christian to be genuinely concerned about the needs of the world and capable of committing himself to do something about them. A childish love will be dissipated in playing pious games; it cannot bear the burdens involved in bringing Christ to the world and the world to Christ.

The mature Christian can never be spiritually isolated. His life is centered in the Church, which is to say, in Christ as he exists in the world. The child lives in his own world, and often in a world of his own making. The youth is self-centered, preoccupied with himself and his own concerns. Only the adult is truly outgoing, centered upon others in a community. For the Christian, this community is the Church. It is in the Church that he nourishes his spiritual life. It is in the Church that he finds the direction of his energies toward his fellows. It is toward the Church that his apostolic endeavors will always tend. Yet, this is not a sectarian interest, a ghetto mentality, or a partisan propaganda. An authentic, mature realization of the nature of the Church and of her mission is as universal and all-embracing as Christ himself. Nothing human is alien to the mature Christian.

An idea fraught with difficulty exists in the realm of authority and freedom. Immaturity is easily discernible at both poles of paternalism and submissiveness. A mature view of Christian obedience will show that it is not an added burden thrust upon us, but rather the perfect way to harmonize the sometimes conflicting demands that are made of them. Here again, there must be a growth toward genuine freedom and toward a self-direction that is guided by an enlightened authority which is not too insecure to trust its subjects.

To achieve mature obedience, the Christian must know the example and teaching of Christ. And to elicit mature obedience, the authorities must be guided by an authentically Christian spirit. Both the governors and the governed must be docile to the Holy Spirit. Both legalism and license must be avoided. Obedience must be seen as a responsibility rather than as an obstacle to freedom. The child and the youth are not prepared to see this. It is a vision reserved to the adult.

The Christian is called to share in the peace and joy of Christ through faith. He is also called to repentance and to the practice of penance. The harmonization of these two aspects of the spiritual life is not easy to achieve. Here, as in other areas of his life, the Christian must strive for maturity. Both overemphasis and neglect of the penitential spirit are childish and destructive of genuine adulthood.

What is involved is more than mortification and the sacrament of penance. The question concerns a general spirit which involves "conversion" in the biblical sense of the word and the development of a true sense of sin. The maturing Christian must grow out of the individualism of childhood notions and the self-centeredness of the adolescent. He must not become fixated on having a "good conscience" at any price. He must come to realize that the very baptism whereby he is incorporated into Christ is itself a "sacrament of penance." He must see that his whole growth in Christ, his life of Christian love, his vocation, his apostolic action, in short, his very Christian being, is a life of penitence. This authentic view frees him from a preoccupation with sinfulness and sets him on a way of self-knowledge enlightened by the Gospel. Along that way he can discover the adult meaning of life in Christ, and he can see that no aspect of his life is without its sanctifying value. Thus, in brief summary does Père Liégé trace the development of Christian maturity in its broad outlines. He writes of truths that need saying and, more importantly, that need heeding. His background and experience both qualify him to speak about his subject.

Pierre-André Liégé was born at Coiffy-le-bas, France, on June 22, 1921. After completing the Baccalaureat, he entered the Dominicans in 1939. He studied at Le Saulchoir and was ordained in 1944. He did graduate work at the Sorbonne and at the University of Tübingen from which he received the doctorate in theology. He returned to postwar France which was seething with religious, political, and social ferment. He began his teaching at Le Saulchoir in the fields of fundamental and pastoral theology. Five years later, in 1951, he began his work as Professor of Pastoral Catechetics at the Institut Catholique de Paris and at the Institut Catholique de Lille. He has since become a visiting professor of catechetics both at Québec and Montréal.

He has been greatly influenced by the thought of his confreres, Pères Chenu and Congar, and he has been actively engaged with apostolic groups of priests, university students, religious, and laymen who work for social improvement. For eight years he was Chaplain General to the *Scouts Routiers de France*. He is coeditor of Parole et Mission, an influential journal of catechetics and missiology published by Les Editions du Cerf. He is a peritus of Vatican II and a consultant to the hierarchy of

Pierre-Andre Liege, O.P.

France.

I got to know this book before I met the author. It was during a year as a Fulbright Research Scholar that I met Père Liégé. He was teaching at the Institut Catholique where my work was centered, and he lived at the Couvent St. Jacques, to which I was attached. During 1963-64 I came to know him well and to admire him greatly. Our conversations served to strengthen my conviction that he is a theologian who faces the needs of the day with a clear insight based on profound learning.

When the rights to make this translation were secured, I wrote that I felt that some of his phrases, like certain French wines, would not travel well, and that I would like his permission to try in some places to convey his thoughts rather than his words. He was gracious enough to allow me complete freedom to endeavor to bring his ideas clearly to an English-speaking audience. It is thus that some of the examples have been altered to make them more meaningful, and that a few phrases have been adapted to make the meaning more clear in our language. I wish to thank Pere Liégé for his permission to depart from the text in places, and I assume full responsibility for whatever changes I have made. My thanks are also due to my friend and colleague, Colman O'Neill, O.P., professor of Theology at the University of Fribourg, for his invaluable assistance with the translation.

St. Paul's stem injunction, "Be a man," comes clearly to each succeeding generation of Christians, and finds each generation in need of special qualities of maturity to meet the challenge of its own time. Père Liégé's ideas will be helpful to all who are seriously concerned about achieving their proper stature in Christ so that they might spread his Kingdom in our day.

Thomas C. Donlan, O.P.
Blackfriars
Chicago, Illinois

PIERRE-ANDRE LIEGE, O.P.

I

Human Maturity and Christian Maturity

The subject of maturity is of great current interest. Articles are written about it both in popular magazines and professional journals. It is frequently the topic for lectures, and it is discussed in ordinary conversations. Achieving maturity poses special problems in the realm of human psychology for those who are increasingly aware of the complexity of modem existence as it creates pressures and tensions in daily life. In addition, there are other problems of a spiritual nature that must be faced by Christians who strive to achieve maturity as they confront the unprecedented demands that they encounter in trying to live meaningfully according to the Gospels in today's world.

This concern with the achievement of maturity is not a mere fad; it is a very real problem that has its roots in a growing realization that many adults prove incapable of coping successfully with their life situations. There is a marked retreat from adult responsibility not only on the human level, but also at the more demanding level of the Christian commitment. Any normal adult who seeks a worthwhile place in human society and in the community of the Church must necessarily pass through the phases of childhood and of adolescence. Modern education must recognize the difficulties encountered in guiding children and youths through the stages of their development toward genuine maturity. It is not enough to discuss maturity in order to acquire it. The attitudes of the young must be carefully developed. Right goals must be proposed to them. Practical guidance and effective examples must be supplied. Otherwise, they will remain stunted. They will never reach genuine adulthood.

Taken in its most complete sense, adulthood demands a certain level of development in both the natural and the supernatural areas of life. What is the relation between human maturity and Christian maturity in those who follow Christ? Do they affect one another reciprocally, or are they rather relatively independent of each other? Can there be a mature Christian who is not a mature human being? This is the basic problem to which we will try to give an answer.

At the very outset an objection may be raised that is so fundamental that the question of Christian maturity may seem meaningless. If the Christian life is a life of supernatural grace, completely and at every moment dependent on God, how can spiritual maturity be dependent upon factors of human psychology? This objection is an oversimplification based on a misunderstanding. While it is true that life in Christ is a life of grace, this does not mean that it is something miraculous or something fatalistically predetermined by irresistible forces. Ordinarily, God adapts his gifts to the capacities which he has providentially prepared in us. For example, God rarely intervenes dramatically with the grace of sudden conversion.

Here Christian maturity will be discussed in terms of the conditions which Providence ordinarily establishes for it. Yet, it must be clearly understood that in so doing none of the elements of maturity are withdrawn from the rule of grace. On the contrary, everything depends upon grace in achieving Christian maturity.

For a beginning, no more is required than to consider the facts of the spiritual life. It is true that they must be explained, but the facts themselves have a certain significance.

First, it is clear that Christian maturity never exists apart from some degree of human maturity, granting that, in some cases, this degree of human maturity may appear before its usual time.

Second, it is clear that human maturity demands a certain degree of Christian maturity, and that this need is far from always being fulfilled. Third, it is clear that we meet defeat whenever we attempt to impose the demands of an adult Christianity on someone who lacks the requisite human maturity.

These facts of the spiritual life point to the adoption of this working hypothesis: Between human maturity and Christian maturity there is neither a mechanical correspondence nor a complete independence, but rather, ideally, a proportionate development.

In order to attain a fuller understanding of these data, it is essential to clarify exactly what is meant by the term "human maturity."

What Is Human Maturity?

There is really no short answer to this question. Rather than try to invent one, let us consider a few of the most relevant facts of psychology and of sociology, which are directly connected with elements that must enter into the concept of maturity.

1. An adult is someone who has achieved a fundamental unity of personality. Unlike sthe adolescent, the adult is no longer in the process of self-discovery and self-realization. All adolescence is a process of developing; an adult is a person developed. Children or adolescents may have known moments of unification in their personalities, but such experiences of maturity would be only provisional, because they would be realized in a personality not fully explored. An adult has a fully explored personality. Adults have discovered all their resources and the worth of each of their faculties. They know themselves. They can concentrate on their powers so as to express themselves and give themselves to others by a completely free act. They have achieved stability in their personalities.

2. An adult has outgrown passing enthusiasms and now lives according to convictions. When we speak of passing enthusiasms, we think first of bursts of superficial sentimentality, like the wild demonstrations that greet some movie stars and athletes. But there are other types as well. There is a kind of fixated enthusiasm which arises from a single clear and inflexible idea, such as we see among the followers of certain political or religious groups. There is the enthusiasm for any activity that brings brilliant or dramatic results, such as are had in politics or in science. Much of this enthusiasm is characterized by an undeniable sincerity, just as most of it lacks complete self-involvement, reflection, and true freedom. This is typically adolescent behavior.

Real convictions are different from such bursts of enthusiasm. Convictions are not necessarily devoid of emotional overtones, but they commit the entire personality, involve freedom, and do both on a permanent basis. Convictions provide truly and decisively the motive for adult living. Mere generosity or activity will not suffice for adults. They must know why and for whom they are so engaged.

Adults realize that they are worth what their hearts are worth (in the biblical sense of that term as it means the center of our spiritual personality). This is the center of the human person. It is more profound than any psychological division between knowledge and desire. It is the place where the most basic questions of life are answered.

3. *Adults recognize that they are responsible for every aspect of their lives.* Their existence as responsible persons is seen as a whole, and as a whole is lived in all of the moments and in all of the events in which it is gradually unfolded. Whereas the adolescent lives by fits and starts, or sees human existence as no more than a series of disconnected events, adults know that they have only one life, and that everything in it holds together. They recognize that they are responsible for the quality of their entire life, and not just for those isolated moments when morality is explicitly considered. They are capable of being loyal to the great, guiding principles which alone give meaning to life and provide that stability which is founded upon convictions

4. *An adult is someone who is aware of the social dimension of life.* An adult is conscious of having roots in society, of being-with-others, and acknowledges that membership in the human family demands a personal concern for others. Adults are no longer self-centered, but open, in a responsible and active manner, to the persons and to the things among whom they exist. They are capable of dealing with the sociological groups and complexes which determine the life of individuals. They are also able to direct their activities toward general conditions. They are not limited to dealing simply with isolated events.

5. *An adult is well adjusted to the realities of life.* As long as we live in an abstract world, preferring dreams, fantasies, or even ideas to concrete daily experience, we are not yet adults. Adults do not try to cheat life. They seek to enter into it in a realistic fashion, accepting its limitations and its setbacks without either being crushed by them or compromising with them. They are even capable of facing up to whatever lack of balance they discover within their own personalities, recognizing it rather than pretending it does not exist. They are down-to-earth, bestowing a measure of dignity on ordinary things. They are above arbitrary choices, above taking flight into a world of fancy, above self-delusion.

Two further remarks must be made after this discussion of characteristics of adult psychology. First, the most rudimentary analysis of the modern world easily shows how much it is in need of adult personalities. Its complexity, its intensified socialization, its accelerated pace, its demands for involvement, its democratization, all of these tend to increase the numbers of the maladjusted and the neurotic among people who have remained in an infantile or adolescent psychological state. In a more simple and peaceful world these people would never have known the same tensions, but neither would they have been required as urgently to achieve maturity.

Second, we are now in a position to apply these traits of the adult personality to living the Christian life. Unity of the personality will be strengthened by making the decision required for a conversion in faith; such a decision involves the whole person at a more profound level of freedom. The discovery of supernatural convictions will supply new, coherent and lasting motives for existence. The invitation and the judgment of God will increase the meaning and the extent of responsibility. Social life will be raised to a new level, one that embraces the entire Church and everything which affects the growth of the Kingdom of God. Acceptance of reality will bring about the genuine humility of the sinner who is saved, and who takes encouragement from the optimism of God himself.

Outline of the Solution to the Problem

Everything that we have seen thus far inclines us to conclude that Christian maturity is certainly conditioned by human maturity, even if it happens that the call to the Christian life is not always accompanied by an adequate degree of human maturity. What has been a hypothesis up to this point will become more certain after considering the following important principles.

1. How could God ignore the important gifts associated with different stages of development of life? If a person's life passes through various stages of personal development; if reflection on the human experience found in infancy, youth, maturity, and old age is so full of meaning; if each of us must pass through adolescence into our mature years, how can we say that it is not normal for God to give us time to progress toward eternal maturity at a pace in harmony with our development as persons?

2. Of all religions, that of Christ is one which makes demands on freedom and on conscious motivation, without bowing to the over facile and spontaneous sources of religious sentimentality and morality typical of primitive or infantile people. It is a religion at once supremely personal and communal. It makes demands on conscience that are capable of decision and well aware of the responsibility. This is a religion in spirit and in truth.

Does that mean that the Christian life cannot be led by children or by adolescents? Not at all. But this life will be led by them only partially while they await the coming of maturity, even though it is lived totally by each one of those, taking into account their limited possibilities. It is because the religion of Christ is so sublime that only too often, in order to "adapt it," to bring it to the level of human needs, we cheapen it.

3. *Beyond any principle there is Jesus Christ himself, whose life and whose actions are our law.* St. Luke the Evangelist did not hesitate to write, in a phrase whic we take seriously: "And Jesus advanced in wisdom and age and grace before God and men" (Lk 2:52). Not only "before men," as though to appear subject to the laws of human development, but also "before God"!

Unlike the apocryphal gospels, the canonical Gospels do not anticipate for Jesus the horror of his major adult decisions. They do not conceal the temptation of Jesus at the threshold of his entry into public life. Jesus went to meet his hour with the full awareness of an adult.

God speaks to us through the God-man after the manner of the gradual pedagogy of the Old Testament. God waits until we are ready before he bestows his predetermined gifts.

With these guarantees, we can affirm with greater assurance that adults will be capable of a full entry into the mystery of Christ. This would be impossible, apart from a miracle, to the believer who lacks such maturity. There are two signs which make this quite clear, although in a somewhat general way:

- Adult Christians will be able to rise above their partial understanding of the Christian mystery as well as above the restrictions imposed upon it by their subjective attitude, by their temperaments, and

by the lack of unity in their psychological makeup.
- They will be able to express more clearly the specifically Christian motivations of their life and their significance, which exceeds any mere relation to their personal needs (theologians would speak here of "the formal motive of the Christian life").

Approach to a Twofold Maturity

If it is granted that a certain human maturity must accompany spiritual maturity, there are consequences in the field of educational technique which follow. Let us state the most evident of them.

1. *It is necessary to assist children–and childish grownups–in acquiring human maturity, so as to create a climate in which they can strive for Christian maturity.* Instead of fearing human maturity, we ought to encourage it, even if this should mean that here and now things would be complicated, and the decision to lead the Christian life rendered more difficult. This is the road toward reality and toward truth.

2. *But what measures should we take to encourage a maturity at once human and Christian?* We should reflect upon human existence and upon the true situation of the world and of persons in their actual condition. Reflection is not everything, but it constitutes an indispensable element in acquiring an adult intellectual and affective attitude.

We should multiply occasions for responsible action so that freedom can be exercised, the habit of decision cultivated, and the complex realities of life courageously faced. We should consciously acknowledge that, within the context of the faith, there are difficulties, setbacks, and limitations.

We should live in the company of authentic, adult Christians. This is no more than very general advice which will be made more specific in the following chapters.

In conclusion, there is need to correct a common misunderstanding of the Gospel. We recall Christ's words: "...unless you turn and become like little children, you will not enter into the Kingdom of heaven" (Mt 18:3). What meanings have been drawn from these words! Yet, the sense is perfectly clear: evildoers, those who wish to dominate rather than to serve, those who refuse to abandon themselves to the arms of God, who turn their backs on the only true life and cannot enter into the Kingdom of Christ. Our Lord takes a child as the model and the symbol of whoever wishes to live according to the Gospel. What is important to Christ here is not the poetic expression or the simple innocence of a child, but rather the openness of his heart. Jesus did not say, "Remain children," but, you who are in fact adults, "become (again) as little children." What he is asking for is the conversion of grownups.

Hence, there is nothing here of sentimentality or poetry about the angelic eyes of little ones. He is speaking about us. To grow up is a risky business but at the same time it is a magnificent task. The child in us is the adult who accepts responsibility, at the same time remaining well aware of the shallowness of human fame, and perhaps in spite of the fact that we have been hurt by experiences of life. Knowing ourselves to be adults, accepted as such by the world, we remain eternally children before God. There is nothing here that can cover up our infantilism, our childishness, our too-prolonged immaturity.

St. Paul, echoing the thought of our Lord, warns us: "Brethren, do not become children in mind, but in malice be children and in mind mature" (1 Cor 14:20). Are we really able to say with him: "When I was a child, I spoke as a child, I felt as a child, I thought as a child? Now I have become a man, I have put away the things of a child" (1 Cor 13:11)? Are there not among us too many childish grownups who in are neither adults nor children?

We must be very cautious not to confuse this message of the Gospel with that of a whole literature of childishness to which it is very common to compare it today. I am thinking of the works of Dostoyevsky and of Saint-Exupery, of films such as those of Charlie Chaplin or of Fellini. The characteristic of this literature of childishness is the idea that we find happiness by fleeing from adult responsibility, whether a child or a fool be put forth as the model. The spiritual child of the Gospels is one who has already reached maturity; the child of this type of literature is generally one who falls short of it.

St. Therese of the Child Jesus, who has been put forth as the author of a childishness filled with the very confusions that we have just now exposed, has herself written in her autobiography these most revealing lines: "I do not know how I deceived myself with the sweet thought of entering Carmel when I was still a very young child.... The good Lord had to perform a little miracle to make me grow up in an instant, and that miracle he performed on that unforgettable Christmas day.... Jesus, the gentle little newborn babe, that night transformed my soul in a torrent of light. On the very night he became weak and suffering for my love, he made me strong and courageous. He armed me with his weapons and, since that blessed night, I have never been overcome in any combat, but, on the contrary, I have gone from one victory to another, and I began to 'walk like a giant.' It was on December 25, 1886, that I received the grace to leave my childhood behind me, the very grace of my complete conversion. We returned from midnight Mass where we had the happiness to receive the strong and powerful God." "Children that you are,' how long will you rest content with your childish ways?" (Prv 1:22.)

II

Achieving Maturity of Faith

There can be no authentic experience and no valid affirmation of Christian maturity which does not presuppose a mature faith as its foundation. Is it not true that many of the difficulties and crises which arise later in life, whether in the ranks of Catholic action, of the religious life, or of the priesthood, can be explained by the weakness of a faith which has remained infantile or adolescent, and hence unable to provide solid motivation for the choices and the commitments which are empty apart from it?

Making use of the analysis of human and Christian maturity that has been set forth above, we will describe the characteristics of an adult faith and explain its demands with reference to the education of self and of others in the way of Christ. The words of St. Paul will guide us in this search: "We may be now no longer children, tossed to and fro and carried about by every wind of doctrine devised the wickedness of men, in craftiness, according to the wiles of error." But, "we all attain to the unity of the faith and of the deep knowledge of the Son of God, to perfect manhood, to the mature measure of the fullness of Christ" (Eph 4: 13).

At the very outset, we must pay heed to two dogmatic principles, lest we see only the psychological aspect of the present inquiry.

1. *Faith is a free gift of God.* We do not become believers or remain so without receiving from a source outside ourselves the call 'to acknowledge the God who speaks to us', and unless we receive within ourselves the power to embrace wholeheartedly the God who reveals himself and who calls us. It is important here to avoid confusing grace with fatalism, the action of God with miracles, and the

workings of divine Providence with the abolition of human responsibility. In each individual case, the grace of faith develops, increasing gradually like our natural qualities. Growth in grace as well as in nature is marked by discernible stages. It is the trustworthiness of God embracing the untrustworthiness of humans. To acknowledge that faith has roots in time and finds its human aspect in untrustworthiness makes no sense whatever unless we presuppose the existence of grace.

2. *Baptism is the sacrament of faith.* Baptism, then, gives the grace of faith even to children. But baptism is also a demand for faith on our part, a demand for a proven and an adult faith in the catechumen who seeks the sacrament, a demand for development of faith in one who was baptized in infancy and who has thus received the seed of the basic capacity for such development. Only rarely does God provide ready-made results. It is less a question of preserving in the faith than of constantly growing in the faith.

Now that we have established the context of our inquiry, we will proceed to develop three ideas: 1) Maturity in the faith implies an adult type of conversion. 2) Such a conversion itself implies an encounter and an identification with the one true God. 3) This conversion brings the entire personality of the believer into the unifying force of the Mystery of Christ.

The first of these points will illustrate what conviction and complete freedom really mean. The second point will illustrate what responsible acceptance of the motivations of life truly implies. The third point will illustrate what a unified and totally committed existence involves. All of these points have been shown previously to indicate the presence of human and Christian maturity.

The Adult Believer Must Be a Convert

We usually distinguish converts from non-converts or those who were baptized in their infancy. This distinction is dangerous, however, because it allows one to think that those baptized in their infancy do not need to be converted. An actual incident will serve to illustrate this point. A group of twenty young adults had just witnessed the baptism of one their friends. His conversion forcibly impressed on them how much the step of receiving baptism means to a man who only yesterday was a pagan, in terms of the complete break with his past and the seriousness of his decision. All of them had been baptized when they were infants, and all had received a Christian education.

The priest who performed the baptism asked them, "Supposing that you were not baptized, could you, in all sincerity, state that the decision of your faith and your engagement to Christ are such that you would not hesitate to take freely this step which has led your friend to baptism?" Only one responded "Yes." The others explained sincerely that their faith did not have the strength of a personal conversion. What was lacking to the faith of these young Christians? Was it not their failure to have entered into the realm of adult faith by means of a personal conversion? This would have brought them from the state of baptized infants to that fullness of baptismal life so admirably exemplified in their newly-converted friend.

What does conversion imply? In order to give a satisfactory answer to this question, it would be necessary to analyze what the New Testament calls *metanoia,* an expression whose richness of meaning is most closely approached by the phrase, "change of heart." Let us recall here its fundamental elements.

In the Gospels, the term "heart" means the very center of the entire personality. It is here that we act and enter into communion with God. It is the focal point for those decisions which engage not only the will but the spirit itself, which commands our freedom and our loyalty. It is the moral conscience seen precisely as the invitation of God and viewed as subject to God's judgment.

In short, before God and before others, we are worth what our hearts are worth. For this reason Jesus will place at the very center of his religious teaching the responsibility which an adult, hearing the word of God, accepts wholeheartedly either for salvation or for damnation. "For where thy treasure is, there also will thy heart be" (Mt 6:21).

When we see the approach of God and hear his voice, our hearts must choose their course. In the words of the New Testament, the heart will then be opened, enlightened, committed, on fire, obedient, sincere, wholesome, expansive, pure, fixed, believing; or else, on the contrary, it will be blind, hardened, unrepentant, uncomprehending, lost in darkness, uncertain, evil, and faithless.

A conversion concerned only with ideas, a change that is merely intellectual, is not the conversion spoken of by the Gospels. By the same token, a conversion which reaches only to the levels of feelings and religious sentiment or which merely adjusts us to our own situation at the ethical level, is not the kind found in the Gospels. Only at the most profound level of our being, with all that goes to make us adult persons, "with our whole heart", can the believer make a decision with regard to the Word of God which searches her out. The heart which receives the Word becomes a heart inhabited by God and by the Spirit. "To have Christ dwelling through faith in your hearts," that is the prayer of St. Paul for the Ephesians (3:17).

In this fullness of meaning, conversion is an embracing, in the sense of a total self-giving, of the new world founded upon the judgments and the standards proposed by Jesus

Christ. It means to take as one's own the idea of happiness and the demands of life which are those of Christ himself. It means to receive into one's very self, "into one's heart," a new mind which is that of Jesus Christ.

The Christian faith is more than an empty, uncommitted acknowledgement of the truth of the Word of God. Involving both the grace of God and human choice, it provides a completely new center for the believer's entire existence; henceforth she will be perfectly responsive to the voice of God. It is our reply to the preaching of the Kingdom. It is our initiation into the world of the Covenant which, since the Incarnation, penetrates the human race.

Whatever degree of union with God we may have achieved, conversion in the Gospel sense of the term always involves a renewal of heart. It begins with the insight of a repentant sinner and terminates with a total personal commitment to Jesus Christ, who has been recognized in and through his signs as the very presence and the salvation of God for everyone who opens her heart to the Gospel message. The New Testament simply makes more precise the nature of this conversion of heart which the Old Testament already places at the center of prophetic preaching.

The mission of the Church of Jesus Christ until the end of time will be to proclaim to all what Jesus announced at the very beginning of his ministry: "The time is fulfilled, and the Kingdom of God is at hand. Repent and believe in the Gospel" (Mk 1:15).

To those Christians already converted, but whose faith lacks vigor and dynamism, the Church must preach conversion in order to stir up a more complete and lasting commitment of their hearts. To baptized children and adolescents, the Church must preach conversion so that a faith which dominates the heart will emerge at an age when their personality is developing toward maturity.

To those baptized adults who are not really convinced and whose religion has degenerated into formalism, the Church must preach conversion in order to draw them out of their childish ways and to introduce them to the fullness of the baptismal life demanded by their age.

Finally, to unbelievers, the Church must still, as in her early years, send forth a call to that conversion which leads to baptism, and must do so with all that missionary zeal which is found in the Gospel of salvation in Jesus Christ. All training in the faith, therefore, must have for its goal that type of Christian conversion without which there can be no spiritual maturity. Such a goal is not achieved in a single day. While it is true that the unification of the personality marked by liberty cries out for this conversion, still it can be said that the child is not yet capable of it, while the adolescent is just beginning to sense its possibility.

The faith of children has its anchor in the environment of the faith in which they live. Their faith is an acceptance of and a consent to the faith of those who surround them, just as their freedom is a sharing in the choices made by the adults upon whom they depends. A test of faith generally occurs for the first time in adolescence when the young balance the faith of childhood against the new personal discoveries of the powers of emotion, of reflection, of ideals, of their bodies, and of their feelings. Will they be carried away by their gradual discovery of their own richness? Will they hesitate to acknowledge Jesus Christ as the master of their lives at the risk of having to renounce the pursuit of these enticing discoveries? Or will they begin the work of their conversion by freely submitting to Christ the depths of their emerging personalities of which they have so recently become aware?

On the threshold of maturity, there is still another test to be undergone, a test that will question the faith of the adolescent in preparation for a new stage of development. This time he will be summoned to weigh the call of God, not only against the resources of his own person, but also against the enticements of adult life which have begun to thwart freedom. These are the satisfaction of work, of love, of having a creative function in a growing world, of being at ease with other human beings.

Will yesterday's adolescent believers, sentimental and idealistic though they still are, attribute to Christ a position of supreme importance in the adult life that is opening up for them? If they do so, it must be through a more determined conversion which will serve as the prelude to the final conversion of their mature years. Will they resolve to belong wholeheartedly to Christ rather than to that pagan world which is open to them? Or will they relegate to some remote corner of their personality the faith of their infancy and adolescence as a kind of insurance against a rainy day? Henceforth Christ speaks in the clearest tones making demands upon their liberty and upon their entire personality. The "heart" is summoned to take its stand and to be converted.

God in the Faith of an Adult

At every stage of life, the Christian's faith has for its motive the God of revelation. For the Christian, to believe in God is always to believe in the God of Jesus Christ, and to believe precisely because of the invitation of the Gospel and the grace of its message. But there are many purely human motives which can lead us to take notice of God. Influenced by these human motives, even Christians under the guise of faith can set up one of strange gods of the philosophers or of the sociologists or of the false religions, a god who has nothing at all in common with the true God of Revelation. As long as the Christian motive for believing in God does not dominate the other motives, as long as the God of the

Gospel of Jesus Christ is not acknowledged in all his uniqueness, there can be no question of an adult faith. The conversion of which we are speaking is a conversion to him whom Christ called, "the only true God" (Jn 17:3).

There are ways of looking upon God which are characteristic of the religion of our childhood. He can be seen as the "God of the primitive peoples," a kind of force acting in and through the world of nature who evokes a holy terror. This God can be seen as the "God of majesty," a sovereign who has need of servants and who imposes obligations. And he can be seen as the "God of a well-ordered society," who guarantees the safety of his supporters and who supervises the policy of human society.

There are also ways of looking upon God which correspond to the religion of an adolescent. This God can be seen as the "God of the romantics and of artists," who fulfills the yearnings of sentimentality and sometimes the need for a religious folklore as well. He can be seen as the "God of moral idealism," who is no more than a supplement to the ideal of gallantry or of good fellowship. He can be seen as the "privately-owned God," a pure spirit who is interested only in the soul of the individual.

It is unavoidable that the faith of the child and of the adolescent should borrow temporarily something of these characteristics. But progress in the faith consists precisely in rejecting as inadequate, if not as false, any commitment which is based principally or exclusively on an inferior motive. Among these inferior motives would be the instinct of religiosity, the mere sense of the sacred, a sense of moral righteousness, a search for human security, or the need for interior peace.

The Christian faith of an adult will be an encounter with the living and personal God who has spoken to us. It will be a meeting with God the Father who, without any trace of paternalism, invites us freely to accept adoption. This is the God of love, who is always gentle, even when he makes demands and passes judgments. This is the God of holiness, who sets our feet on the way toward a superhuman destiny and a new kind of happiness. This is the God of the Kingdom, who is present in the world, where he accomplishes his plan with our cooperation.

It is important to be very clear about the distinction between faith and the sense of religiosity. The latter can exist either at the lower level of religious instinct or at the higher level of religious sentiment, or, indeed, at the level of the natural virtue of religion. Although we are naturally religious, we are by no means naturally believers or Christians.

This sense of religiosity is strengthened by whatever is sacred and which, under different forms, offers a kind of awareness of a supreme being, of security and of salvation, in spite of our own limitations, our setbacks, and the uncertainty of life. This need for the sacred in one's life and this sense of religiosity are at once both positive and negative influences on the recognition of the absolute superiority of the Christian faith. These influences are negative to the extent that a religious person would run the risk of being content with faith in a mythical God. They are also negative to the extent that we would be satisfied with a kind of Supreme Being from whom we seek nothing more than the fulfillment of our natural quest for human completeness.

When the God of Revelation intervenes in our lives and calls us, it is precisely to question the direction of this same natural quest for self-realization. This is not done in order to deny self-realization, but to enlarge and purify and make it grow, and to invite it to exceed itself by entering into the divine plan. God does not want simply to assist us to reach beyond our self-assigned goals; God builds upon the dissatisfaction within our hearts, confronting us anew with the question of happiness and of our personal and collective destiny. Even if we should succeed in achieving the most complete human happiness, God would still have something to say to us, and the faith would still retain its full meaning, admitting no compromise with religious sentimentality.

For this reason the first Christians called themselves "believers." They wished to distinguish themselves from the pagans (who were, nonetheless, for the most part, religious people). This shows how deeply they were convinced that the Christian faith begins an entirely new and different kind of relationship with God. Whatever is good in superstitious practice or magic rights finds its echo in the true faith which, however, far surpasses and purifies them. Surely the faith has nothing to fear from the disappearance of certain superficial or childish forms of religious practice identified with a particular culture, historical situation, or psychological state. When religious instinct suffers a decline, this is often the moment for the rise of genuinely Christian faith and of a sense of the presence of God that is more authentically Christian.

The Christian sense of God goes hand-in-hand with that adult faith which, under the form of a personal conversion, establishes the beginning and the lasting source of holiness. All the saints have gone through their adult conversion to the God of Jesus Christ in the uncompromising form in which he appears in the Gospels. Thus it was with Francis of Assisi, seeking at last in God the glory which he had previously sought among men. So it was in the dark night of the spirit of Pascal: "Thy God will be my God. Forget the world and everything that is not God. He can be found only along the paths marked out by the Gospel. The joy of his discovery brings me even to tears." Here we see an unconditional choice of Jesus Christ who is the witness to the holiness of God, and here we find a complete commitment to the spiritual ideas of the Gospel.

What do we need to stir up the dormant faith of adult believers? We need educators who are also prophets of the God of Jesus Christ. In the name of the purity of the faith, they must denounce unceasingly those false concepts of God which, like so many foreign and even pagan elements, have insinuated themselves into their own thinking and into the thinking of others in the Church, and which manifest themselves in the common expressions of our faith in God. They must battle incessantly to reestablish purity of motive in the faith against the subtle temptations of magic, of idolatry, of a man-centered devotion, and of unrealistic thinking about God. This was the work done by all of the saints and prophets of the biblical tradition. Educator-prophets such as these ought to have a place in our seminaries and in our novitiates.

The Unity of Mature Faith

The third characteristic of adult faith is that it seizes upon the complete being of the believer and, in turn, is seized upon by the believer in its entirety. It thus becomes the source of unity in his whole life.

1. *The unity of the world of faith.* Adult Christian should have an answer for everyone who asks, "What does it mean to be a Christian? What do Christians believe?" They should be able to do this in one or two simple statements. Most Christians are embarrassed by such a question, because they do not understand what they recite in the Creed. The analytical approach of the catechism has given them only a disconnected series of "mysteries." They cannot see the connection among the various articles of faith, nor the different value and importance that is accorded to each article within the whole. Unfortunately, their religious

conscience is an undigested mixture of dogmatic propositions and commandments. A faith which is mature should provide positive remedies against such incoherence for two reasons.

First, the Creed is a unified whole. There is only one mystery, and that is Jesus Christ. Every article of faith expresses one aspect of this unique mystery. The different aspects must be always related back to their center which is the love of God for us being manifest in the history of salvation, God's plan for his creation, the Paschal Mystery of Jesus Christ, which is the central event of all history, and the Kingdom of God which is being built by Jesus Christ. Just as human love allows us to understand from within the coherence of the behavior of the person whom we love, so also faith permits us to understand the coherence of the different aspects of divine revelation. Everything holds together because God has acted with the coherence of love in the history of salvation. Adult faith takes for granted that one has begun to assimilate the Mystery, and that one has penetrated into the reality which underlies the Church's expression of faith.

Second, adult believers must therefore be on their guard against giving equal value to all the teachings of his faith. For instance, the Kingdom is more important than hell, grace is more important than sin, the Holy Spirit is more important than the pope, and Christ is more important than the Blessed Virgin. This will lead them to assign each article of faith to its proper place. They will neglect none of them but, at the same time, they will not allow themselves to be led astray by their personal inclinations, nor by any enthusiasm of mind or heart, nor by the uncontrolled multiplication of private devotions.

2. *The unity of faith with life.* A faith such as this will open to the believer the real world of the living God who is actively present in history. A faith like this has no trace of escapism

into the realms of false mysticism or abstract thinking nor any trace of that craven fear so often found in the consciences of the uninstructed or of the romantic.

Such a faith brings an exact recognition, definite and unequivocal, of the identity of Jesus Christ. But it is never reduced to a theoretical or merely verbal "orthodoxy" of those who parrot the Creed as they learned it from some teacher of religion.

Such a faith will guarantee a special kind of coherence to the believer's behavior, and it will guarantee that she will not remain inactive. Her observance of the commandments and their cooperation in the apostolate, consequently, will not be mere external appendages. Each aspect of revelation must have a significant impact in his life. The fatherhood of God becomes the basis for fraternal charity, the resurrection of Christ for the Christian use of the flesh, the communion of saints for life in the Church, hell for the mature use of liberty in the sight of God, and so on. This overall unity of the faith with personality, brought about by conversion, branches out and embraces each detail of the Creed so that no article thereof remains an empty abstraction, but becomes a vital force for Christian living. Little by little everything takes on new life. The assertions of faith come alive, and this life makes these affirmations real. For the baptized Christian, life is nothing other than the progressive conversion of every aspect of life into the reality of the Mystery which is seen in the light of faith.

Such a faith blooms in the Church of believers as in its normal environment; it allows faith to be truly personal without having to be isolated; and it allows faith to be shared without degenerating into mere good-fellowship. It is capable of bearing witness without adopting either the intolerance of the crusader or the indifference of the libertarian. The missionary spirit is part of its very nature.

This is not simply a question of technique, but of interior life. It is folly for us to think that we can become adults in the faith without a total effort on our part, an effort which takes as its source a serious dedication to Christ, a dedication that is constantly being tested and constantly being renewed in act. Adulthood requires more than generosity of spirit and a degree of liturgical practice or a theoretical study of religious topics.

Adulthood cannot rest upon the single prop provided by the sociological climate of traditional Christianity. These reflections on mature faith give rise to certain practical directives which will conclude this chapter.

I. *What is required is reflection on the Christian message of the Scriptures.* This must be more than an attempt to increase religious knowledge. It must be a serious meditation which brings about a progressively more intense participation in the indispensable dialogue between God and humans. It also requires a battle against spiritual sloth, and against the superficial attitude of the well-wisher and the do-gooder. A certain amount of theological study is absolutely necessary, but it must always be an answer to and a prolongation of personal meditation. We should be able to say, "I am a believer," and not simply, "I have a belief." Such an answer indicates that we really live by faith.

2. *The second requirement for adult faith is reflection upon the daily experience of life and on the problems besetting the world so all of this is seen in the light of faith.* We must reflect upon our behavior and upon our activity. Only on this condition will action nourish and deepen the personality of the believer. It is by knowing the truth and by doing it that we enter more fully into the light and reality of the Christian world.

It is also in this practical sort of reflection, in the light of the Word of God, that the life of the Christian is purged of childish dependence on feelings or surroundings, of pharisaic or pietistic formalism, of false mysticism, and of merely human motivation. By such reflection Christians will always be prepared to meet successfully whatever objections may be raised against them by the non-Christian humanists of our day.

3. *The third requirement is an active and personal participation in the liturgical life of the Christian community from which the faith draws its nourishment.* We are speaking here, of course, only of a genuine liturgical piety and not about superstition or empty ritual. The Christian liturgical mystery admits of no compromise. It is a constant restating of the very heart of the faith, and it draws the believer into a mystery which is realistic.

4. *The great problem posed by contemporary atheism can, in some cases, compel Christians to become more mature in the faith.* This is no place for the unprepared to venture alone. Today we find certain kinds of atheism which are reactions against childish forms of religious practice. Simple refutation is not the answer. Adult believers must strive to provide a living reply to this kind of atheism in their own Christian lives.

PIERRE-ANDRE LIEGE, O.P.

III

Achieving Mature Charity

We will speak here of fraternal charity. It is not our intention to write a theological treatise on this subject, but rather to show how the quality of human relations demanded by Christian love supposes, and indeed causes, a certain maturity of personality.

If we condemn childish and juvenile types of affection which hinder charity from achieving its full maturity, this is not a denial but an affirmation that the essence of charity is supernatural. Because it is a purification and a transformation of our relations with others, charity requires a certain refinement of the human powers of communication. But of all the forces of the human personality, the affections require the most time for development. Maturity of the affections calls for a more fully developed charity and, at the same time, is presupposed by this very development.

Furthermore, the more we lack a solid theology of charity, the more we may be deceived by confusing a general feeling of good will toward others with true charity. Adolescence is a time of sentimental generosity. Highly emotional and complicated temperaments, characteristic of people who have very strong passions, seem to be endowed with a natural generosity. Does this mean that in such cases charity will be a natural gift? It is necessary to investigate further by going beyond the merely psychological plane.

Let us try to evaluate the most certain signs of Christian maturity in human relations. To do so we will make use of some of those traits which we have already seen to be indicative of human and spiritual maturity. The principal characteristics that we shall investigate here are: conscious motivation of behavior; unity of personality; adaption to social conditions; and the courage to face reality.

The Maturity of Charity and the Motives Proposed by the Gospels

"That love which inflames the devout Christian," writes Bergson, "is not simply the love of man for God; rather it is the love of God for all. In God and through God, the Christian loves all people with a new love. This is not the brotherhood which philosophers have urged in the name of reason, by arguing from the nature shared by all men in common. One must bow respectfully before an ideal so noble; one will even put it into practice if it is not too embarrassing for the individual and for the community; but one would never be passionately devoted to it" (*Les Deux Sources de la Morale et de la Réligion,* p. 250).

When we recognize God as Father according to the teaching of the Gospel, we enter into the world of all-embracing and active brotherhood. It is because of what we believe that we give ourselves more generously to the service of others. God the Father and Jesus Christ are the reason for his love, and they, too, determine its measure. Generosity, whether it be due to age or temperament, needs to be "baptized." It can be considered as a providential basis for charity. But is it not true that this generosity is more often spontaneous than deliberate, more enthusiastic than controlled in its impulse, too much the slave of instinct to be universal?

Everyday experience shows that natural generosity does not always accomplish what it intends, despite the evident sincerity of the person. We often meet people who harbor a hard core of egoism that is never completely overcome, and others whose good intentions are never realized because they are overly sentimental, and still others whose enthusiasms blow hot and cold.

This does not mean that even a conscious and active espousal of the Gospel ideals will bring about radical transformation in one's temperament; what it will do is draw us out of ourselves and place effective obstacles to our becoming self-centered. Those whose adolescent enthusiasm has died down or who are of a more low-key temperament and who, too easily perhaps, regard themselves as irreformable egoists, can actually cultivate a genuine charity if they adopt these ideals. There are many individual forms which Christian charity can assume and, consequently, many different vocations, but all find unity in the single motive proposed by the Gospels, without which there can be no question of true charity.

It is evident how much each of us can benefit from a knowledge of our own individual temperament in our struggle to achieve maturity in charity. Such knowledge enables us to master our temperaments rather than to be mastered by them. This self-control is not really possible except to a grownup. The emotions of adolescents are too turbulent to allow them to achieve it. But the education of adolescents ought to prepare the way for charity. Let us remember that St. Paul tells us that the only thing of any value in the sight of God is that "faith which works through fraternal charity" (Gal 5:6).

The Maturity of Charity and the Unity of the Personality

To enjoy an effective relationship with another in the most universal way possible, and to unite the world of human relations with the world of grace and of Christian endeavor, a person must already have achieved a basic integration of the tendencies and powers within the self. There must be a certain autonomy of the self if there is to be adult communication with others.

Here we are touching upon the central problem encountered in achieving the maturity of the affections. One who has not won emotional independence from parents runs the risk of remaining childish in an important area of relations with others. Certain ties of childhood must be cut if new ones are to be established in adulthood. One must progress from a situation of being totally dependent on the few toward a situation of being able to share oneself with the many.

It is generally recognized that this transition will be made successfully in the measure that we are able to live truly *with* others rather than simply to live *in their midst;* in the measure that one feels the need to be *with* others rather than feeling the need *of* others or the need to be *for* others. Clearly this is a matter of dominant traits which increase, but never to the point of excluding the satisfaction of personal need. The total sharing of self with others is an ideal as unattainable in this life as the pure and disinterested love of God. But there is still place to adopt the terms of psychologists and to speak of the well-grounded personality in terms of a transition from the stage of possessiveness to the state of disinterested love.

We can easily find concrete examples in observable behavior of childish traits which are so harmful to charity. One person has need of repeated and assuring signs that he is understood in order to be emotionally secure. This can go so far as to produce a rejection complex. Or we might question whether others like us, or unconsciously multiply our futile attempts to please others, or withdraw behind defense mechanisms for fear of showing ourselves to be what we really are. It is easy to imagine how such childishness sets limits to the possibility of meeting and communicating with one's neighbor face to face.

What remedies must be sought? Leaving to the psychiatrist the sphere of mental illness, we ought to encourage whatever will promote self-reliance: true appraisal of one's self and one's worth, with neither false humility nor self-inflation; the possibility of achieving self-confidence, and freedom from infantile dependence; an atmosphere of frankness in human relations, setting aside a slavish following of group patterns, of customs and manners of speech; the experience of intentional silence and of withdrawal from the crowd.

It is only in adulthood that one can truly realize this unification of the self which conditions the honest recognition of another as a person and of one's relationship to her. An evident clarification of this is found in the relationship between man and woman in love and in sexuality. How can one who is not unified in his own personality bring to sexual life that element of self-surrender which must be incorporated into a creative union between two persons? Anarchy is introduced into sexual relations when no account is taken of the personalities involved, and when this relationship is degraded by participants to the level where it is no more than a means of winning the most superficial and irresponsible kind of self-assertion. On the contrary, the charity uniting a Christian husband and wife demands adult responsibility in their interpersonal relations. This is only one case. Every relationship based on adult charity, if it is to be authentic, demands a unified personality.

Christian educators should strive to bring about this unification of personality precisely because it is necessary for a life of charity. Are they sufficiently concerned about this?

The Maturity of Charity in the Social Dimension

The process of finding one's place in society, which is characteristic of adulthood, progresses through stages marked by changes both in social circumstances and in our reactions to them. The intense subjectivity of early childhood gives way to a period marked by a more balanced recognition of elements outside the self. This more balanced outlook in turn seems to be threatened by the recurring individualism of early adolescence. But shortly there is begun a new phase of social living that is more controlled and more personal than the crude sociability of later childhood. It is thus that one approaches an adult social life where we harmonize the most acute personal awareness and the broadest appreciation of the social dimension of individual existence, in tune with the situations and the commitments of maturity. Anyone who would choose to remain locked up and blind to the complex network of human relations within which they are involved would betray their immaturity. And the same thing may be said of those who would seek principally in social life a means of escaping from themselves. This phenomenon is sometimes observable in certain Catholic activists.

This adult attitude toward society is an indispensable condition for acquiring a true appreciation of the Church. This is a matter to which we must return later. It is in this very complex network of interpersonal and intercommunity relations that the fate of the Gospel is worked out, and in which the kingdom of grace is extended. One clearly sees that the social world of the adult supplies to the exercise of charity its most advantageous field of action. This is particularly true in times such as our own when the increasing complexity of civilization leads to a great strengthening of the sense of human solidarity. Charity is practical. It really works. It must express itself in the existential situation in which we find ourselves, developing in step with the great collective egoisms which it has the duty to conquer. Nothing can be more opposed to an adult charity than a superficial conscience filled with good intentions, but lacking a deep understanding of those causes of evil which Christian love must oppose.

The charity of which we speak is not ingenuous. It is not the possession of "gentle souls," but rather of those great hearts who understand the needs of their times. In our time charity has become more demanding than in the past, because it is true that each day sees yet another realization of our yearning for solidarity with one another.[6] "No one can any longer with good conscience ask the question which the lawyer of the Gospel addressed to the Divine Master two thousand years ago: "And who is my neighbor? Our neighbor is every man; the Central African or the Indian of the Amazon forests hoping for spiritual goods much more than for material goods" (Pope Pius XII).

We can develop people who will be serious about the responsibilities of charity by lifting their sights above their limited horizons so that they may get to know the true situation of others in the world today; by not neglecting to ponder the condition of their neighbors (this amounts to having at least a minimum of political awareness and refusing to pass oversimplified or prejudiced judgments); by struggling against that infantile complacency that is found in doing those customary but no longer relevant "works of charity"; and by recognizing all the good there is in social institutions which are springing up everywhere instead of disdaining them.

The Maturity of Charity and the Acceptance of Realities

Every day adults are confronted with the realities of life and of human relations. As long as we live in the world of childhood or adolescence, we cling to some remnant of unreality. This occurs much more commonly with a

---

[6] Editor's note: See Thomas Merton's account of his mystical experience at the corner of 4th and Walnut in Louisville, Kentucky, where he saw himself as radically related to those around him in *Conjectures of a Guilty Bystander* (New York: Image/Doubleday, 1966).

temperament that is a little bit sentimental, and which keeps alive the illusion of a sugar-and-spice world inhabited by people who are gentle and kind. Adults must practice charity in the concrete conditions of life where they deal with real people and actual groups. Without betraying its nature, their charity cannot ignore the difficulties, conflicts and the blunt talk that is sometimes necessary.

At this point we must dispel a few confusions. Charity does not consist in avoiding every disagreement with everyone. It must not be confused with the spontaneous mildness of an unruffled personality. It never dispenses with courage in the defense of truth. For the adult, the hard reality of charity is the enemy and the calumniator whom one must be willing to pardon for the love of Jesus Christ, for it is in adulthood that enemies are inevitably made, and that one encounters misunderstandings. The hard reality of adult charity is the swarm of critics that we risk bringing down upon our head by taking the part of the poor, or by disturbing the established order that protects the privileged few.

Christians must have learned at the feet of Christ himself to be meek and humble of heart – which by no means rules out violence either in defense of the oppressed or wherever truth and justice are at stake. They must have learned to love their neighbors even though a particular one be worthless and a sinner, and to love them without cynicism or discouragement. This by no means excludes a realistic appraisal of the people concerned. We must have learned to understand the beatitudes of the merciful and the peacemakers, knowing all the while that we may be misunderstood. We must have learned to speak the truth at whatever cost whenever love requires it, putting our own interests in second place.

Only adults have the patience and the strength of character necessary for the constant effort required to achieve good human relations. We do not confuse open discussion and differences of opinion with hostility. We have grown out of the stage of *passing enthusiasm* to enter that of *commitment.* Mature charity cannot be discussed without using this word. For as long as we are able to retreat, as long as we have not burned our bridges behind us, we have not really given of ourselves totally. On the contrary, when we commit ourselves, we force ourselves to persevere in the works of charity, and we cast aside the capricious choices, the dreams, and the pretexts which are so many aspects of that basic egoism which never completely dies.

A charity which is too easily discouraged, which asserts itself only on special occasions, which is full of good intentions that never quite reach the skin of a humanity that is uncomfortably close, a charity which picks and chooses, a charity which will not dare take a risk: is this the charity of an adult Christian? It is well to read the answer given by St. Paul (1 Cor 13).

The truth is that wherever human experience grows in depth, it raises a cry for a charity that is more inspired by the Gospels, that is more personal in its relations, that is more expansive and all-embracing in its works, that is more courageous and more trustworthy in its battles.

IV

Growing Spiritually in the Church

Christian life is always life within the Church. Beginning with our first act of faith, the Christian enters into and accepts the Covenant, the place where the Word of God is spoken. At no moment can the Christian conceive of any union with God that is independent of the Church – the only place where such union can be achieved. The Church is not an extrinsic element appended to some Christian act; rather it is intrinsic to it from very inception.

In the experience of most Christians, the discovery of this fact is slow to come, at least any conscious discovery which becomes a part of our interior spiritual life. Everyone admits that childhood and adolescence are periods of life that do not favor a proper appreciation the life of the Church. And this brings us again face-to-face with the theme of spiritual maturity. Everything happens as if a certain degree of maturity were necessary to give full value to life in the Church of Jesus Christ. If we recognize that the mystery of the Church, more than any other, requires for its understanding practice as much as instruction, he will not be surprised to discover the relationship between maturity and full participation in the life of the Church. To be able to think and to feel *with* the Church is a great deal more than simply to know a few things *about* the Church.

Among the criteria of human and spiritual maturity set forth in the first chapter of this book, it is quite evident that "adaptation to social living" will highlight the Christian meaning of the Church in a special way. We will consider first of all the stages, from infancy to maturity, of this adaptation as it pertains to life in the Church. We shall then turn our attention to the question of motives, the ability to work with groups, and the acceptance of reality.

Integration into Social Life and Awareness of the Church

In any analysis of what it means to live in the Church, we cannot avoid separate considerations of the two elements which make up the Church of Christ on earth: the interior reality through which the eschatological community takes shape and the institutional and sacramental structure that mediates this interior life. This does not mean that we are separating the two elements in the Church. These are two aspects of one and the same Church. All we wish to do is to indicate that the believer encounters the Church under these two aspects.

The Church is an Eschatological Community

It appears that the Christian child has very little difficulty feeling at home in the Church under this aspect. However, his participation cannot be either very complete or very deliberate. The child, far from being by nature an individualist, has a spontaneous sense of belonging to a religious group. It is by virtue of this inclination that he takes part in the life of the community. But the child is still very far from recognizing this group as the assembly of those personally summoned by God who are on the way to becoming saints and with whom Jesus Christ fills his Kingdom.

This spontaneous sense of belonging to the Church which we find in the child must ripen and deepen through the faith until it becomes the free and deliberate adherence of the adult believer. This transition will generally not occur without a salutary crisis of development, the sort of spiritual growing pains that we observe in many of our young people.

The young Christian discovers the essentially personal character of the faith and realizes what is meant by saying "I believe." Loyalty demands that we examine the reasons for our belief. Young people undertake this search as private individuals, often unaware of the fact that it is actually taking place within the fold of the Christian community. Furthermore, they fear the herd mentality of a faith that relies on community existence, and they criticize the faith of their own childhood for having had this very weakness. Contrasting their own need for personal conviction in the faith with acquiescence in the belief of the group, they are not far from complete individualism in the Christian life. And it will generally be by joining some little group of young people, or by coming into contact with some particular priest, that they will retain even a minimal tie with the community of the Church.

Maturity will let them survive this crisis. We have seen how this works out on the natural plane. How many of us must await maturity before we can understand our precise relation with our families and with our country? Following the instinctual attachments of childhood, there come the critical moment and the search for independence that characterize adolescence, a period during which all earlier ties are strained to the breaking point. But there will come a day when adults will freely embrace the communities into which they were born. This will be in a manner marked by a free and deliberate attachment inspired by gratitude, devotion, a sense of justice and of social responsibility.

Since the social qualities of the adult believer are elevated through the Holy Spirit, Christians can combine the most intensely personal faith with a profound realization of membership in the communion of saints. They will discover that the Church is not simply a sociological group, nor a party, nor an army, nor a religious sect, but rather a community in the full sense of the word, made up of believers who have been personally called and sent together on the way to glory by Jesus Christ.

In the light of this understanding, their true relationship with the community of the Church will become clear. They will see that the community is not a substitute for the person, but rather that it will demand more in the way of personal commitment to the faith. It is not something placed at their service as though they had no more to do as Christians than to make use of the Church for their own interests. The community embraces every facet of their personal relationship with Jesus Christ, and it calls upon them to leave behind an egoistic search for the assurance of a merely individualistic salvation.

The Church as the Institution of Salvation

It is easy for Christian children to submit to the direction of the Church and its representatives, because obedience and dependence are familiar elements in every phase of life. In their young eyes, the priest possesses an authority even more unquestioned than that of his parents and teachers. The whole aura of authority which surrounds the priesthood and the sacraments strengthens this idea of an unquestionable authority of which God himself is the source.

The transition must be made from childish submissiveness to a free and responsible acknowledgement of an adult dependence on the apostolic authority through which God bestows his gifts on us. Generally, this will not take place without passing through a period of turmoil in the faith.

Young Christians will be tempted to transfer to the authority of the Church, which protected them during their childhood, all of those sharp demands for independence which have turned them against all those who cared for them and instructed them. In the measure in which submission to the Church appears as a more or less human and sociological phenomenon, they will criticize it as something childish, as the enemy of freedom, as an unwarranted intrusion on their privacy, and as a mere formalism. At the time when they discover their personal worth, it will be difficult for them to see the connection between this worth and the very institution which even now is the object of their accusations. It is not easy to understand this crisis of growing up, and it is better to let it play out over time rather than to impose a solution by force.

Adult Christians will find in their own mature faith the resources to reconcile these conflicts. Their acknowledgement of the authority of the Church will be motivated by the Word of God rather than by any human assurance. Their obedience will not reduce them to silence nor to the eradication of their critical faculties, nor to a state of passivity. Neither will the power of criticism lead them to revolt or to discouragement. Once again a measure of psychological maturity corresponds to a deepening of the faith. Is it not the mark of an adult to listen to the advice of others before coming to decisions and before carrying out his plans on his own responsibility? On the contrary, children allow themselves to be led hither and yon, and adolescents think they are capable of piloting their own ships without assistance.

Is it not the mark of mature persons that they can accept obedience as a necessary condition for sharing in social life, and as a means to discharge their social responsibilities? Is it not part of adult realism that we see that the noblest human hopes and ideals must depend on some tangible external expression if they are ever to achieve any personal or social value? Adults are never ashamed of their dependence on material signs and things.

In the development of Christian social life, then, we can observe the contrast between youth and maturity which are the steps by which the adult Christian enters fully into the life of the Church. Although many baptized Christians are born into the Church, they live and die without ever having truly become members of it. Very often they remain fixed in a childish state of passivity which, while preserving them from difficulties, also prevents them from developing in the faith of the Church of their birth. Others are arrested at an adolescent state in a defensive attitude toward the Church, as though they dwell at its outer perimeter and fear to be exploited by it.

Thus, we may conclude that there can be no Christian maturity without a free and deliberate participation in the Church into which one is born by baptism, and without accepting the responsibilities of full citizenship in the Church of which one has been an adopted child since infancy.

Motives for Living in the Church

The Church can be found attractive at the human level even by those who are not believers. From this level derive many of the natural attractions which can influence some to accept Church. The Church will be praised for its moral and civilizing function, for its sense of discipline and of authority, for its power, for its beauty and good order, for its traditional stability, and so forth. There is nothing abnormal or unworthy about this so long as such motives remain secondary, dominated by the faith which alone can explain exactly what the Church of Jesus Christ is. But if this natural attractiveness, which is so congenial to certain temperaments, to human enthusiasms, to sociological needs, or to personal prejudice, should come to be the dominant or exclusive motive for belief, the Christian meaning of the Church itself suffers. Spiritual maturity must bring to bear on this problem the clarity of the true faith, which throws sharply into relief the total superiority of the Church when it is compared to any other society that bears some resemblance to it.

The Church can exist only in dependence on the Lord Jesus Christ who gathers it together in the Holy Spirit. All the human elements in the Church have been given a new meaning by Jesus Christ. The Church cannot be explained by anything merely human. Nothing dominates the Church, with the single exception of Jesus Christ who alone has the right to the "cult of personality." Adult Christians look to the Church for what it alone can do, for what it alone can give, the very things for which it has been created and sent into the world: the Gospel, the

Covenant, the holiness of Jesus Christ.

Only this attitude of faith makes it possible to distinguish in the life of the Church what arises from human *traditions* and what arises from divine *Tradition*. We can't lift a finger to tamper with that Tradition without separating ourselves from Jesus Christ. In a society characterized by respect for tradition, which is the expression of a stable world, there is a tendency to identify *Tradition* with *traditions*. The rapid pace of change in a time like our own, when traditions are being uprooted, lays upon us a special obligation to clarify and to purify motives for belonging to the Church. Faith should permit each believer to encounter the express will of Jesus Christ who is the very fountainhead of the Church. Beyond any arbitrariness, beyond any empty legalism, beyond any utilitarian concern for human security, there are motives of Jesus Christ himself, which must become the motives of his followers. His is also the source of true freedom for the Church, for by appearing in her own true colors and being recognized as such, the Church needs only the truth as its justification. It has no need of political maneuverings, of human craft, of reactionary fear, of worldly servility, of craven self-abasement, unlike those other societies which are wholly at the mercy of human events.

In short, a mature appreciation of the Church will show believers why they should suffer and, perhaps, even die for the Church, no longer identifying her with any human ideal, but rather with Jesus Christ their Savior. To know what is worth giving one's life for is true freedom.

Toward a More Catholic Appreciation of the Church

Human maturity expands our horizons and lets us find ourselves at home with others. Christian maturity will transform these capacities into a more catholic appreciation of the Church. How will this take place?

By an existential dialogue at the very heart of the Catholic community, believers will become aware that they are not by themselves the Church. This dialogue will take place between the hierarchy, who witness to the coming of salvation through the mediation of the sacraments, and the laity, who witness to the coming of salvation through the mediation of history. The dialogue will take place between the Church of contemplation, which witnesses to the already eschatological character of the Kingdom, and the Church of the apostle, which bears witness to the still missionary state of the Church. It will be a dialogue which respects and sees the need for different vocations, different ministries, and different responsibilities. There will be no place for rivalry marked by petty jealousies about power or privilege. For the Church of Christ is never identified with any national church, nor with any single parish, nor with any particular movement, nor with any individual pope, nor with any group of laymen, nor with any particular religious order. The lack of Christian maturity has too often been characterized by provincialism, narrow sectarianism, and parochial bickering.

The Christian adult will find in truly Catholic expansiveness a sense of true unity. This will be a unity which does not close its eyes to differences, which does not equate itself with mere uniformity or regimentation. It will be a maturity that is practical without being over-centralized; it will be a unity which will not cower before the inevitable differences and divisions met in life, because it recognizes that these can enrich it so long as its living principle is the Holy Spirit. Uniformity is closed in upon itself; unity is open to embrace diversity.

Life in the Real Church

It would be an error to mistake the foregoing reflections for a description of life in the idealized Church, a life which agrees completely with the will of our Lord, a life that will exist only in the heavenly Kingdom. At the same time that it recognizes the divine character of the Church, Christian maturity must allow the believer to face all those things in the Church which bear the stamp of history and of human weakness. The divine comes to us through the human. This Christian maturity must be based on a very humble acceptance of the mediating function of the hierarchy and the sacraments, both admirably adapted to expressing salvation in its historical dimension. It must be based on a humble acceptance of the conditions which affect them at any given time or place. Christians will not be scandalized if there is too much of the human element present at certain times. They will analyze the real reasons without pious deceit, and at the same time will not defend whatever may be wrong. They will not regard these mediations as some kind of magic formulae, because they will understand how much responsibility and seriousness of faith they require on the part of their ministers. This is at the opposite pole from a lust after miracles which would have the Holy Spirit always acting beyond the limits of his ministers, and even in spite of them. The Holy Spirit is be more respectful of the order of Providence.

Mature Christians are prepared to accept delay, hesitancy, and weakness in the life of the Church. Surely they will suffer from them, and there can be no question of defending them. But we must remember the mercy of the Savior for his people. Do not all in the Church say the Confiteor together? Christian criticism can only be inspired by faith and by love without bitterness or rancor. Only those who are truly committed to the Church's struggle against sin, and who hunger and thirst for the holiness promised in the Gospel have the right and the duty to offer criticism.

In the last analysis, everything is resolved for adult believers in the fact that they belong to a Church which they know to be the Kingdom and which they also know is not yet so. They live by the hope of the Church. They long for the coming of the Lord, and work with all their might to hasten it.

PIERRE-ANDRE LIEGE, O.P.

V

Christian Maturity and Obedience

There are many different forms of human obedience. There is the obedience of the child, of the soldier, of the citizen, of the employee and so forth, all of which result from different personal or social situations. Although everyone must be obedient to some degree, it is clear that all obedience is not equally helpful nor equally mature.

Solely from the point of view of human maturity, some criterion should be established to indicate the existence of adult obedience. Children are submissive rather than obedient. Their dependence is too spontaneous to be either free or deliberate. Their willingness to be led is more easily explained by their lack of personal initiative. This submissiveness has nothing to do with the virtue called "docility," but is more akin to the automatic responses of a well-trained animal.

It is difficult for adolescents to achieve obedience as it is measured by objective standards. Having rejected infantile slavishness, they do not willingly accept a position of dependence except upon those who command their admiration, enthusiasm, or attachment. Clearly, then, only in adulthood are they able to pass beyond the conformism of a child which for all its objectivity remains slavish, and the obedience of the adolescent, which is both subjective and arbitrary. Full entrance into social life, an ability to judge motives, a sense of responsible decision, these are the signs of the presence of maturity. They make us capable of a more satisfying obedience, compared to which we must say that many kinds of obedience actually practiced by people who are no longer children are, in fact, childish.

Does Christian obedience have anything in common with childish types of obedience? Some seem to think so, because they denounce the immaturity sometimes observable among the faithful, particularly among religious who are vowed to the practice of obedience. Pius XII admitted that this was a real danger, but he went on to define the ideal in the following words:

> Is the religious life an obstacle to the proper development of a human personality? Is it true, as some suggest, that it canonizes childishness? Let us look with an unprejudiced eye upon the behavior of men and women who belong to the states of perfection. Certainly no one would dare to state that the majority of them suffer from immaturity in their intellectual and emotional life or in their actions. In the First Epistle to the Corinthians, St. Paul rejects as alien to Christian adults, ways of thinking and feeling which are proper to the child. Let each member of the states of perfection, whether superiors or subjects, apply the words of the Apostle to themselves. Then every danger of immaturity will disappear, without diminishing respect for lawful authority or sincere acceptance of its decisions" (*Address to the Second Congress of the States of Perfection*, December 9, 1957).

All too often genuine Christian obedience has been confused with forms of obedience that are too narrow even from a human point of view. Christian obedience has been interpreted as little more or less passive than the obedience of a child, or as the more calculating obedience of a soldier, or the obedience forced by social conditions upon unemancipated children or servants. It is important to find out whether or not the motives for the Christian virtue of obedience that are proposed in the Gospels are not better affirmed and carried out by more mature types of obedience. If it should turn out here, as on the other points we have touched, that Christian behavior implies a certain degree of human maturity, and indeed awakens and develops it, then Christian obedience will emerge in all its grandeur. At the outset, we must discover the principles and motives that elicit the obedience of the Christian. This will enable us to examine the exercise of obedience both in those who obey and in those who command in the name of Jesus Christ.

The Sources of Christian Obedience

Christian obedience can be understood only in terms of supernatural faith. Human motives are not sufficient to account for it. Christian obedience is part of that world of which Christ himself is the Law.

1. The obedience of Jesus Christ. The whole life of Jesus was an act of obedience to his Father. This is the basis of the entire Paschal Mystery. Jesus had no desire to lead a life based on self-will, or to taste the satisfaction of a will independent of God. He neither did nor said anything of himself independently of his Father, and as his hour approached, he entered more profoundly into communion with the divine will. It was at Calvary more than at Bethlehem that Jesus was perfectly obedient (see Phil 2:5-12).

But note immediately that the surrender of his own will coincides in Jesus with a completely free and responsible submission to the will of his Father. This is most clearly seen in the episodes of his temptation in the desert and at Gethsemane. There is nothing about Christ which would suggest the fabled victim ground inexorably under the irresistible power of an arbitrary God. His Father's demands are meaningful for him personally. It is within the compass of the vast plan of God that Christ asserts his liberty, confident always that in God there is nothing arbitrary, nothing absurd, nothing inimical to our freedom. This is why the obedience of Jesus can be understood only in terms of our dedication to the divine will, a dedication offered by a mature heart in the clear light of his unique divine calling. To interpret such an obedience in legalistic or even ascetical terms would be to debase it; for, even though it passed through hours of darkness, it is in the light of the Covenant that it had its motives. The entire Gospel of St. John should be read with this in mind.

2. The terms of Christian obedience. "Thy will be done on earth as it is in heaven." This will is perfectly revealed in Jesus Christ and in that new and eternal Covenant of which he is the author and of which the Holy Spirit is the life-giving soul. Here obedience is given only to the Father, to Christ the Lord, and to the Holy Spirit. All the forms and circumstances which affect Christian obedience are ways of obeying the Holy Spirit who is the source of the holiness and of the public mission of the Church. Whatever goes by the name of obedience in the Church has the unique purpose of making us obedient to the Spirit. Christians obey the Spirit, and not laws or commands of any sort. St. Paul tells us: "Walk in the Spirit...if we live by the Spirit, by the Spirit let us also walk" (Gal 5:16, 25).

Aquinas echoes this idea: "The principal element in the law of the New Testament, and that whereon all its efficacy is based, is the grace of the Holy Spirit, which is given through faith in Christ" *(Summa Theologia, I-II, q. 106, a. 1).* All the written directives and commands are secondary. Commenting on St. Paul's phrase, "the letter kills but the Spirit gives life" (2 Cor 3:6), Augustine remarks that the letter denotes any written law that is external to us, including the moral precepts of the Gospel (see I-II, q. 106, a. 2). The letter of the Gospel itself would be deadly were it not for the interior presence of the healing grace of faith.

All obedience to the Holy Spirit is clearly identified with the life and growth of the Kingdom, where alone it finds its meaning and its fruitfulness. This is a life of obedience, modeled on that of Jesus Christ. Like that of Christ, the obedience by which believers submit to the Spirit implies a clear faith and a personal commitment. One can be obedient only to a person. The Spirit issues no edicts, rather, he appeals to the heart; he opens our eyes; he gives the power to fulfill his commands. His compulsion is all from within. This is why St. Paul insists: "Understand what the will of the Law is" (Eph 5:17) and "seek how to please the Spirit." Mute passivity and empty conformity are alien elements in obedience to the Spirit. What is called for is the greatest measure of free and responsible submission, together with personal acquiescence.

To obey the Holy Spirit is to be free. To limit one's obedience to external laws, even the laws of God, is to renounce personal integrity. Once again St. Thomas remarks that whoever avoids evil, not precisely because it is evil, but by reason of a command of the Lord, is not free. On the contrary, it is they who avoid evil because it is evil who are free. It is here that the Holy Spirit works, perfecting our spirit interiorly and imparting to it a new energy. As a result, we will avoid evil because of love, just as if it had been commanded by divine Law. In this fashion we are free, not that we are outside of the divine Law, but because our interior spiritual energy brings us to do whatever the divine Law prescribes (Commentary on II Corinthians, chap. 3, lesson 3). Forced obedience, therefore, can never be Christian obedience, the limitless demands of which are the very root of the believer's freedom.

3. *The meaning and function of authority in the New Covenant.* The obedience which leads to the Spirit finds its external expression in space and time through the Church's life. Christian obedience must have an exact assessment of the means through which it is exercised. It requires faith in the authority of those who have been established by Jesus Christ to rule the flock in the Holy Spirit. Consequently, it is necessary to remember that, in Christian society, no one apart from Jesus Christ and his Spirit has a right to a "cult of personality".

Leaders are servants of the Spirit, and brothers of those whom they have the responsibility to lead along the ways of the Covenant. The leaders can lay no claim to personal dominion over the flock. "Feed *my* lambs" and "On you I will build *my* church," Christ said to St. Peter. And St. Peter says the same thing to the bishops who are his brothers: "Tend the flock of God which is among you, governing not under constraint, but willingly, according to God; nor yet for the sake of base gain, but eagerly; nor yet as lording it over your charges, but becoming from the heart a pattern to the flock" (1 Pt 5:2-3). Paternalistic authoritarianism hardly squares with that very significant episode of the washing of the feet (see Jn 13). If a leader has authority in the name of the Spirit, it is to lead others to obey the Spirit, according to the purposes of the Spirit, without eliminating the Spirit on the one hand, and without forgetting the discretion of the same Spirit on the other. He is no more than a servant, consecrated or installed to do the work of the Spirit for the sake of the faithful (Lk 22:7-11; 22:24-28; Mt 23:8-13).

The Mature Exercise of Christian Obedience

The precise meaning of Christian obedience depends both on the superiors and on the subjects. Each group must bring to it a mature attitude. There are innumerable cases where the exercise of obedience is unnecessarily disturbed, if not rendered impossible, because either subject or superior has remained stunted in an immaturity which vitiates either the authority of the one or the submission of the other. For although the virtue of obedience is primarily a virtue of the subject, the Christian virtue of the superior has an important role in evoking it.

This brings us to an examination, in the light of the principles set forth above, of the need of a mature obedience on the part of those who obey and on the part of those who command in a Christian community.

1. The Mature Conduct of the Superior. First of all the superior must strive to interiorize true principles of Christian obedience. This will eliminate all aggressiveness and every inclination to resort to force in dealing with his subjects. For all are alike are under the influence of the Holy Spirit whom the superior must be the first to obey. An awareness of working with the Holy Spirit will forestall the superior's demanding obedience solely in the name of self-denial, with no other value than an empty conformism and the bending of the will of the subject. As in the case of the obedience of Christ, Christian obedience may not always give its reasons, but it never degenerates into arbitrariness and empty formalism.

A superior has need for great humility when called upon to interpret, with a view to the common good of the Kingdom, the will of the Holy Spirit in changing circumstances. In this search for the will of God, it would be wise to invite the cooperation of those to whom the interpretation of that will is directed.

The superior's purpose must be to lead subjects to maturity rather than to humiliate them; to lead them to act responsibly, and not to destroy their initiative. An obedience which virtually excludes initiative, which dictates down to the least detail the goals to be sought and the means to achieve them, effectively impedes maturation. Good superiors desire to elicit a self-reliant and constructive obedience. They know that God does not want a slavish conformism, and that he values only the service of those who stand free and on their own two feet.

Finally, the Christian superior recognizes the area of uncertainty which nearly always surrounds most carefully-weighed decisions, and the risk of not heeding the inspirations of the Holy Spirit as intelligently as would be desirable in someone possessing authority. Should the case arise, she will do penance for it, rather than give way to annoyance or make excuses.

It hardly need be said that only a Christian who has reached a minimum degree of spiritual maturity will be able to exercise such a difficult ministry and become the teacher of others in the matter of obedience.

2. *The mature conduct of the Christian subject.* Obedience reveals to the Christian the ways of the Holy Spirit. These are the ways of the greatest demand and of the greatest promise. They require

the greatest generosity in whoever would travel them. There is no way in which obedience makes up for immaturity, indecision, timidity, or the desire to have a good conscience at a bargain price. Serious adults who need an escape from fickleness, and who seek a total commitment of life, should concentrate all forces through obedience, so that they may find a defense against their own inconstancy and laziness, against the uncertainty of an attempt to discover the will of God by one's self

How could such an obedience be other than loyal? How could it be anything less than an internal response to the inspirations of the Holy Spirit recognized in the commands of another? Obedience which seeks only to conform to a rule with a minimum expenditure of intelligence, freedom, and personal involvement is childish. Obedience which knows itself to be responsible even as it submits is mature.

Adults become capable of facing up to the realities of life, putting aside all dreams and fancies. Even when authority is imprudently exercised, and when the human elements obscure the role of the Spirit, mature persons are not unduly disturbed. They know how to cope with human inadequacy without abandoning their habitual obedience, even if they have to make certain adjustments. Adults trust their superiors, and this attitude leads them to cooperate in moments of difficulty. If in some serious case they must have recourse to a higher superior, they do so out of concern for the common good of the Kingdom, loyally without seeking personal vindication. What we have been trying to say is that, unlike the child or one who has remained immature, it is the adult who is capable of living out fully a life of Christian obedience.

We are concerned essentially with evangelical obedience as it is carried out in a Christian community. More precise applications would have to be made for those who live a religious life under the vow of obedience, taking account of the different schools of spirituality and the different types of religious life. While the essentials of obedience are common to all, there are certain shades of difference, for example, between the obedience of the monk and that of the nun, between the obedience of a priest and that of a religious sister.

Although it exceeds the limits of these reflections, it could also be made clear precisely in what manner the Christian obedience we find within the supernatural community of the Church can and should be extended to the obedience which ought to exist in the natural communities of the family and the nation. Certainly the spirit of evangelical obedience should contribute to these human forms of obedience which too often lack any genuine spirit. There are cases, of course, when faith will lead us to condemn certain unreasonable excesses of authority, for, as the apostles declared before the Sanhedrin: "It is necessary to obey God rather than men" (Acts 5:29). Christian obedience does not accommodate itself to sociological preconceptions of what it ought to be. Rather it seeks to bring the spirit of the Gospel to these ideas and, as a secondary result, to make them human.

PIERRE-ANDRE LIEGE, O.P.

VI

The Spirit of Penance in the Mature Christian

It is evident that a spirit of penance is a fundamental characteristic of the Christian life. The difficulties begin once this general statement has been made, when one is asked to spell out exactly what is meant by the spirit of penance. Is it an act of mortification or renunciation? Is it the act of the sinner in the sacrament? Or is it a more general movement in the life of one who has been converted to Jesus Christ? Or are all these various aspects linked together?

If one considers mortification to be first in importance, as common usage suggests, the question is not answered because of the different ideas and different practices which penance implies. The same penitential practices are adapted for different reasons due to different temperaments, different upbringing, to non-Christian influences of a religious, moral, or philosophical nature. Even aesthetic or romantic ideas influence these practices, especially among adolescents. There is certainly a need to give a truly Christian definition of penance.

The facts of the matter suggest a hypothesis. If the confused motives and ambiguous ideas to which the name "penance" is sometimes applied seem to be more frequently encountered during the unrealistic stage of adolescence, is this not a sign that a direct relationship exists between spiritual maturity and the penitential behavior that is specifically Christian? Psychiatrists are unanimous in teaching that at times certain mental or emotional disorders are concealed beneath the façade of penance in the lives of some Christians. Christian practice can sometimes unintentionally provide a justification for the masochism which seeks an almost erotic satisfaction in suffering, or the problems of an unhappy and disturbed conscience, or a tendency to seek failure and persecution in life.

Our hypothesis finds confirmation in the light of Christian teaching. The various aspects of Christian penance are grouped in the New Testament around the term metanoioa, or "conversion." In this context each aspect finds its unity and its true meaning. We have seen that conversion is a fundamental expression of maturity in the faith. Is this not a confirmation that Christian penance requires a beginning of spiritual maturity if it is to be practiced in its fullness and in the spirit of the Gospels?

What is the exact place of penance as an element of the *metanoia* of the Gospel? This must be our first concern. Afterwards it will be possible to state more precisely the nature of the adult sense of sin, the adult manner of using the sacrament of penance, and the adult approach to mortification.

Throughout these reflections we will make use of the following criteria of mature behavior: freedom from dependence on passing enthusiasms; responsible exercise of freedom; willingness to criticize one's motives; the acceptance of reality; full entry into social life.

The Metanoia of the Gospels and Penance

"And after John had been delivered up, Jesus came into Galilee, preaching the Gospel of the Kingdom of God, and saying, 'The time is fulfilled, and the Kingdom of God is at hand. Repent and believe in the Gospel'" (Mk 1:14-15). This call to conversion, linked to the announcement of the Kingdom and to belief in the salvation of Jesus Christ, constitutes, according to the New Testament, the key to Christianity. There is no other gate by which one may enter. Consequently, it is impossible to devote too much time or too much energy to the consideration of the idea of "conversion of heart" in its Gospel meaning.

Difficulties begin with the very translation of the Greek term *metanoia*, which the authors of the New Testament use. This term, so rich in biblical overtones, is only imperfectly rendered by "repentance," "renewal of spirit," and "penance," which are commonly found in various translations. "Conversion," even in the more precise form, "conversion of heart," remains somewhat ambiguous. In light of all of these unsatisfactory attempts to translate the term *metanoia*, perhaps it would be preferable to introduce the Greek term itself into our language. Literally, *metanoia* signifies a change of outlook. It means nothing less than the passage by a person called by God from a world without salvation into the world of salvation in Jesus Christ. *Metanoia* is used in the New Testament to signify at one time the entire process, and at another, one of its stages or elements; at one time God's call to conversion, at another time the response of someone under the influence of grace. It may be the first conversion, at another time the conversion which takes place after a lapse; or sometimes a more intense conversion.

But, in any case, the process comprises three stages: the first stage is the grace of enlightenment; the second stage is the grace of repentance or penance; the third stage is the grace of union. It is possible to limit the term "conversion" to the third stage, on the condition that it be understood that there cannot be any conversion which does not include enlightenment and penance. Or, as we shall do, one can understand conversion of heart to include the entire movement of *metanoia* in all three stages, which are linked together in one vital process.

1. *Conversion as enlightenment.* We have spoken of the grace of enlightenment. This does not mean an enlightenment about our state measured by human criteria that we can discover for ourselves. It means, rather, a perception of our spiritual need and of our sinful state in the light of the revelation of the God who has called us to holiness. Faced with an understanding of what life in the Covenant requires of us, and of the kind of existence into which God wishes to introduce us, whatever may have been our former relations with God, we pass judgment on ourselves as we truly are. Formerly I knew I was a sinner, now I *know* that I am a sinner. This is indeed a grace, for the God who

infused a new enlightenment and a genuine humility in me did this only in order to lead me to salvation.[7]

It is to the Jews first that Jesus, following the example of John the Baptist and the prophets of the Old Testament, addresses his call to penance. They were aware of the demands of the former Covenant. They could enter into the Covenant which was possible to me only by leaving behind their complacent consciences and by allowing themselves to become convinced of their spiritual poverty and of their sinfulness.

Jeremiah, speaking for God, reminds the people of their unfaithfulness to the Covenant: "I kept sending you all my servants the prophets, telling you to turn back, all of you, from your evil way; to reform your conduct, and not follow strange gods or serve them, if you would remain on the land which I gave you and your fathers; but you did not heed me or obey me" (Jer 35:15). John the Baptist preached to the multitude: "Bring forth therefore fruits befitting repentance, and do not begin to say, 'We have Abraham for our father'"(Lk 3:8). Addressing the Pharisees, Jesus said: "The men of Nineveh will rise up in the judgment with this generation and will condemn it; for they repented at the preaching of Jonah, and behold, a greater than Jonah is here" (Mt 12:41).

On Pentecost, Peter said: "Repent and be baptized every one of you in the name of Jesus Christ for the forgiveness of your sins"

---

[7]Editor's note: Once again Flannery O'Connor offers a striking example. In her short story "The Artificial Nigger," she describes the conversion experience of Mr. Head, who "had never known before what mercy felt like because he had been too good to deserve any, but he felt he knew now. ...Mr Head stood very still and felt the action of mercy touch him again, but this time he knew that there were no words in the world that could name it. ...He stood appalled, judging himself with the thoroughness of God, while the action of mercy covered his pride like a flame, and consumed it. He had never thought himself a great sinner before but he saw now that his true depravity had been hidden from him lest it caust him to despair. (*The Complete Stories*, New York, 1979, 269-270)

(Acts 2:38). Sharing in the salvation of Jesus Christ presupposes the admission of one's state of unfaithfulness to the God of the Covenant, a state one is powerless to leave and which one is barely able to perceive.

But what is penance for those who do not know God and who have not been beneficiaries of the Covenant? God makes himself known in his own way. He has spoken to every heart. For these also, a certain awareness of sin is the beginning of conversion. This may be no more than a recognition of the inefficacy of own search for happiness, sparked by first hearing the word of God. After having accused the Greeks of their forgetfulness of God, St. Paul concludes: "The times of this ignorance God has overlooked, but now he calls upon all people everywhere to repent; inasmuch as he has fixed a day on which he will judge the world with justice by One whom he has appointed, and whom he has guaranteed to all by raising him from the dead" (Acts 17:30-31).

For Christians as well, penance begins by an enlightenment on the state of their own lives, having as its criteria Jesus Christ and the conformity that a life once converted should have with the Gospel. To the church of Ephesus, the Apostle sends this message: "But I have this against you, that you have left your first love. Remember therefore whence you have fallen, and repent and do the former works." (Rev 2:4-5). And the prodigal son said: "Father, I have sinned against heaven and before you. I am no longer worthy to be called your son" (Lk 15:18).

Thus, it is always in relation to the call of the Holy God and to the world of covenant and conscious of our own weakness that we are caught up in the movement of Christian conversion. The awareness of sin will be more or less clear according as one has already known Jesus Christ. For it is in relation to Jesus Christ and to the harmony of the new life into which he intro-duces his followers that sin appears in its true light. "No one who abides in him commits sin; and no one who sins has seen him, or has known him" (1 Jn 3:6). But sincerely to recognize that one is a sinner in the light of Christ, is already to have set foot on the path to full conversion.

2. *Conversion as penance.* Incipient conversion calls for action. The awareness of sin would serve no purpose if it did not bring about a change. Penance must be done. Jesus, after John the Baptist, and Peter after Jesus, all preached penance. "I have not come to call the just, but sinners to repentance" (Lk 5:32). It would be a mistake to interpret this call to penance as if it were a simple appeal to a change of behavior and a return to the moral law. All of us are asked to bring forth the fruits of repentance in the presence of God and because of his Kingdom. This moral change is valueless unless it springs from a repentant heart.

Penitence consists in disavowing one's former life and making up for its mediocrity by a spiritual effort. It is completely animated by a desire for another life, a life according to God, and by the resolution to place no obstacle to it. It is purification rather than mortification, a purification which leads to the goal of conversion where the repentant heart, having turned away from its life without God, begins to turn toward God who awaits it.

3. *Conversion as a movement toward God.* Enlightenment and penance make up the negative side of conversion of heart; they are aroused by a positive summons of Jesus Christ to a holy life and to salvation. Penance has no meaning by itself. Its whole meaning is that of a point of departure toward the complete faith proposed by the Gospel.

To be converted, therefore, is to accept, by means of a total commitment, the world of judgments and values proposed by Jesus Christ. It means to accept the idea of happiness and the demands of a life lived according to Jesus Christ. It means to welcome into one's very being, into one's heart, a new mentality which is that of Jesus Christ. It is, in other words, to make the act of faith.

The Christian faith is more than an intellectual acceptance of statements made about God. No doubt it includes an accurate intellectual knowledge about the true God who is identified with Jesus Christ, but it must be a knowledge that involves the entire personality of the one who believes in God. At once the fruit of divine grace and of human decision, the faith establishes a new center of existence for the believer who henceforth must be obedient to the summons of God. Faith is our response to the announcement of a Kingdom; as such, it is our entry into the world of the divine Covenant which has been spreading throughout humanity since the Incarnation.

It is the Gospel, the Good News, which brings us out of false security and summons us to penance. It is the Gospel which brings the movement of penance to its perfection by making it burst out into the new world of faith in Jesus Christ, the world of salvation. The cry of the converts of Jerusalem after they had heard St. Paul describe the baptism of Cornelius now takes on its full sense, "Therefore to Gentiles also God has given repentance [*metanoia*] unto life" (Acts 11:18).

At whatever stage of union with God one may be, the conversion spoken of in the Gospels is always to be seen as a renewal of heart, which begins with the enlightenment of the repentant sinner and leads to a personal and total commitment to Jesus Christ. This renewal is recognized in and through his sacraments and his preaching as the presence and the salvation of God for everyone who opens his heart to the invitation of the Gospel. The New Testament does no more than clarify the nature of this conversion of heart which the Old Testament already placed at the very center of the prophetic preaching.

4. *Christian life is a life of penance.* The process of conversion, which has chiefly occupied us up to now, leads us from the state of complete unbelief to a wholehearted commitment to the Christian faith. This is what one may call "fundamental conversion," or conversion in its pure state. This is what is meant among Christians when they say that someone has received

baptism as an adult: he is a convert. But one must not believe that it is a privilege reserved to the baptized when they are adults to be the only converts in the Church. Every baptized child must ratify the commitments made at baptism, and this is done by a mature conversion.

It can also happen that, after being converted, even sincerely, a believer can deliberately turn away from God and reject God. A believer can return to God only by a second conversion. Even when there is no full rejection of God, but only an indifference and a halfhearted loyalty to him, there is place in every believer who is aware of his weakness, for a continuing conversion. This takes the form of a constant effort to pass from a life where God is only inadequately known to a life more intensely Christian where he is more fully known.

Without denying the distinctions we have made among the elements of Christian conversion, one is justified in saying that the penance preached in the Gospels constitutes the very foundation of adult Christian life.

Penance in the Gospel and the Mature Sense of Sin

The enlightenment of the repentant Christian implies, as we have seen, a true awareness of his sinful state. But such an awareness is never found in a child. Let us give some general idea of how it may be acquired. The moral conscience of a child is naturally concerned with objective right and wrong. This child's world is divided into what is permitted and what is forbidden, into reward and punishment, all of which are neatly fixed by laws and commandments. Children are inclined to be more aware of breaking a law than of committing a sin.

Children must not be allowed to remain in this undeveloped moral condition which is hardly distinct from that of any non-Christian child who has been well brought up. How is one to pass from this idea of rule-breaking to the idea of sinning? By introducing the idea of the God of Jesus Christ, not only the

God who is the Sovereign Legislator and the Judge of Actions, but the God who invites us to share a new life with him. This is the God whose laws are in no way arbitrary or harsh. What he asks of us is our cooperation in our own betterment. He is a God whose majesty is that of a merciful father.

It is important to give this Christian dimension to the conscience of children in order to prepare them for future life. While still very young, children should be introduced to those ideas which will flower into a mature and Christian sense of sin. They should be taught that sin is an obstacle to the development of the Kingdom, that it is completely opposed to a fullness of life, and that it is a rejection of Jesus Christ. Preoccupation with law-breaking will be reexamined as they grows older, and the danger is that it will then appear to them as something completely irrelevant to life. The alternative is that immaturity be unduly prolonged, with the result that they will retain in adulthood a childish moral conscience preoccupied with infractions of the law – a phenomenon that is not rare among Christians. How else could we explain the fact that otherwise well-balanced adults confess, for example, of having neglected to say their evening prayers, or of having contradicted their parents?

These examples should make teachers aware of the extreme care that they must exercise not to allow their pupils to confuse the Commandments which express God's will with polite social customs and regulations which express the human will. It is not right to invoke the authority of God to get a child to give his parents a few moments of peace.

Considering the adolescent next, we find youths who already know what is meant by a disturbed conscience. They have discovered within themselves a variety of attractions and needs. Their sense of sin must be related to this new source of morality rather than to external laws. At this stage, awareness of failure is predominant in their conscience – failure against self, against ideals, and against a code of honor. Such an awareness of failure, bringing with it feelings of shame and a resentment of personal inadequacies, sometimes comes close to discouragement.

This shift toward personal moral emphasis is unquestionably a stage of spiritual growth in the adolescent. But it will be such only if they do not fall victim to it; this would happen if they were to transform it into narcissism, focusing exclusively upon themselves, being hypnotized by failure or by grieving over it to the point of despair. Here again, the adolescent's awareness of failure must be developed into an authentic sense of sinfulness. Three steps lead to that goal.

First, adolescents must be brought to understand that, seen in the light of faith, the attraction they feel for their ideals are, in fact, personal invitations from Christ. They must see themselves as somehow belonging to God and to Christ.

Second, to broaden their moral horizon, which runs the risk of being limited to the sole function of curbing emerging passions – particularly in the domain of sex – the ideal that should summon up the best that is in the young Christian is the majestic plan of God in Jesus Christ, a plan for universal love. The principal objective of their moral effort will be to open themselves to others, to place their young personalities at their service because of Christ. In this way, their efforts to bring their instincts under the control of reason will take on a truly Christian meaning.

Third, they must be led to see the full dimension of God's pardon. If Jesus Christ helps us to discover our sins, it is only in order to show us that he is ready to forgive them. He forgives us if we trust him. The adolescent must be brought out of preoccupation with emotions and with self. The first step is not to encourage these qualities, as one might be tempted to do.

It is precisely through failure to put aside childish things at the time of adolescence that so many adult Christians have remained immature in their moral conscience and in their sense of sin. Hence the confusion of sin with an awareness of personal failure, the confusion of shame with sorrow, the preoccupation with the shamefulness of sins of passion, and the pharisaical complacency in one's own goodness. It is fortunate indeed when no subconscious morbidity, the great enemy of real internal liberty and of morality, takes possession of the conscience. This state is too often seen in many Christians.

"And you know that he appeared to take our sins away, and sin is not in him. No one who abides in him commits sin; and no one who sins has seen him, or has known him. Dear children, let no one lead you astray. He who does what is just is just, even as he is just. He who commits sin is of the devil, because the devil sins from the beginning. To this end the Son of God appeared, that he might destroy the works of the devil. Whoever is born of God does not commit sin, because his seed abides in him and he cannot sin, because he is born of God. In this the children of God and the children of the devil are made known. Whoever is not just is not of God, nor is he just who does not love his brother" (1 Jn 3:5-10). With these words of St. John we are at the very heart of the Christian and adult reality of sin. Let us see what they mean.

1. *"No one who sins has seen [Jesus Christ], or has known him."* Therefore, sin appears as a personal infidelity that destroys our intimate union with Jesus Christ. Every sin is opposed to faith (in the biblical sense of the term) in Jesus Christ and in the Covenant. While sinners may retain their faith, they act against it.

2. *"Whoever is born of God does not commit sin, because his seed abides in him."* John is speaking here of what would be the normal logic of life in Christ. This life is nothing other than the development of a divine seed (the Holy Spirit, grace, a Christian conscience), which progressively takes possession of the whole of life and each of the elements of human experience in those who have accepted it by faith in Jesus Christ. Sin is a living inconsistency with the total plan of God and with the total mystery of Christ which make up the world of the believer.

3. *To be a child of God is to lead a holy life, to imitate the holy*

Christ, to love one's neighbors. Sin is opposed to all of this. It is not simply opposed to laws, not even to divine laws. It is not simply opposed to an ideal, however generous. If we are to understand the true enormity of sin, we must have grasped that God is holy, that Christ is holy, that the Christian is called to be holy like God in imitation of his leader, Jesus Christ.

So whenever I sin, I shake off the hold Christ has upon me and I reject the inner law of the imitation of Christ which should inspire my entire existence. I even go against myself as God would have me to be; I set myself against God's design for the universe which should govern my whole life. The Commandments that I kept as a child, the internal inspirations which I followed as an adolescent, were no more than partial expressions of the Christian vocation which is now mine as an adult. Its demands increase until at last they embrace every detail of my life. Whoever has not felt the inspiration to enter evermore deeply into life with Jesus Christ, the Mediator of the holiness of God, cannot understand the nature and gravity of sin. "For you were once darkness, but now you are light in the Lord. Walk then as children of light...testing what is well pleasing to God; and have no fellowship with the unfruitful works of darkness" (Eph 5:8-11).

The Adult Christian and the Sacrament of Penance

What baptism was once for all sinners, the sacrament of penance will be each time the baptized sinner repents of infidelity to conversion and desires to be converted again. It is something like a baptism that can be repeated. It is not enough for sinners to return to God in the secret of their hearts. The return of a prodigal son must be made public by the Church and sealed by the sacrament. What, inversely, would be the meaning of the sacrament of return if we did not decide to turn our hearts once again toward God and toward the word of the Covenant? The sacrament of penance is the sacrament of life for one who is repentant and converted. It is the sacrament which either restores or strengthens the life of grace in the soul.

Sometimes there will be a question of a second conversion in the strict sense of the term. The baptized Christian has reverted to pagan ways, and has wandered far from God the Father and from life in his home just as the prodigal son once did. In former times the discipline of the Church required a prolonged and often public test of sincerity before reconciling the fallen Christian. More frequently, however, there is a question of a second conversion in a broad sense. Christians remain committed to the life in Christ which they accepted at the time of his baptism. But perseverance grows weary, small infidelities are multiplied, and the original fervor grows cool. Regular renewals become necessary in order to arouse the initial vigor. A deliberate return to the first *metanoia* will recapture the enlightenment, will strengthen the spirit of penance, and will obtain the grace of forgiveness and of a more fervent following of the life of Jesus Christ in his Church.

Confession. Just as the first conversion of an adult includes a desire for baptism, the second conversion of a baptized member of the Church must include a desire for the sacrament of penance. It is as useless to approach the sacrament of penance without the intention to become converted as it would be to accept baptism without faith.

We must see clearly the precise meaning of going to confession. In the sacrament of penance the return of the prodigal son is celebrated in and by the Church, with the priest being both the minister of Jesus Christ and the official witness of the Christian community. The penitent comes to express, to formulate precisely, and to submit to the judgment of the Church, that desire for conversion which is already in his or her heart. They are aware that they are sinners, and they come in answer to the call of the Holy God who alone can turn human hearts. They will have either readjusted or completely redirected their lives, so that they are on the way toward a new state.

All of this reaches its conclusion in the sacrament of penance where we confess of sin, profess sorrow, and make a firm purpose of amendment. The essence of the whole event is that the pardon of God is received through the absolution of a priest. The absolution witnesses to the constant faithfulness of God to his Covenant in Jesus Christ, and it renders this faithfulness active in favor of the repentant sinner. It seals the reconciliation and confirms the grace of conversion at the same time that it guarantees the penitents that they are not deceiving themselves about the state of their souls.

Just as baptism is the visible sign of our entry into the Church, so also the sacrament of penance is the visible sign of our reentry into the Church, for we have separated ourselves from her in the same measure that we have separated ourselves from the God of the Covenant. Once the connection of the sacrament of penance with the interior spirit of repentance, with baptism, and with the world of the Covenant has been seen in the light of faith, the use of this sacrament will not become a matter of mere routine or a morally-conditioned reflex. It will protect us from possible neurotic disturbances. Going to confession must be an adult action, an action of real significance, and not simply tidying up of one's conscience.

2. *Forgiveness.* Unlike the Puritan, Christians have no interest in sin for its own sake. We look upon sin with the eyes of God and of Christ, as we have already seen. But there is more to it than this. It is God and Christ who forgive sin. "I believe in the remission of sin," we say in the Creed. Christ has delivered us from the torment of sin. An adult Christian awareness of sin involves certain consequences regarding the penitent's use of the sacrament.

First of all, the general movement of conversion is quite a different thing from personal or social remorse. It is different, too, from resentment over a blow to one's pride. It is different from discouragement. These are distinctions which often are not well made during adolescence. Looking into himself, the prodigal son said: "I will get up and go to my father, and will say to him, 'Father, I have sinned against heaven and before you'" (Lk 15:17). There you have it. Contrition involves a judgment on the inconsistency of one's life as it is seen in the light repentant of faith, a disavowal of this inconsistency, and a decision to return to Christ with the desire of being more faithful to him. The Holy Spirit may sometimes give the special grace of a feeling of sorrow or of the gift of tears to the repentant sinner. But we must not confuse this supernatural gift with those cyclic outbursts of emotion or of anguish which are the result either of age or of temperament. A good proof of this is found in the fact that spiritual sins, which are the most grave, only rarely give rise to the sense of shame or of torment.

Confession is not the sort of compensation that the legalistic conscience seeks so that things may be put in order once more, or that the morbid conscience seeks in order to find peace. Here the word of Christ is what counts, a word that the sinners believe is able to create a new heart in them on condition that they act sincerely and that they enter into the rite of the sacrament with all their strength. It is a sacrament and not a magical rite.

This leads us to distinguish further, in sacramental absolution, the difference between peace resulting from the forgiveness of Christ and that purely emotional feeling of relief from guilt. To improve production in certain factories, managers sometimes employ industrial psychologists who function somewhat like lay confessors. Their function is to give psychological relief to the employees simply by listening to their troubles. The sacrament of penance is not a psychiatric technique, and one should be careful in explaining it not to insist too much on whatever purely human effects it may produce. Its meaning is in terms of a relationship with God and with Christ. We know that sometimes the Holy Spirit gives a supernatural experience of peace in confession, but the word of pardon brings with itself its own certitude and its own reality, which are quite independent of any sensible experience. Surely it is not necessary to insist that this purely psychological feeling of deliverance suffers from the limitations of guilt feelings, the shame of which we have spoken above. The essential thing is that there should be an effective change in the life of the forgiven sinner who proposes to enter more and more fully into life as a convert.

Practices of Penance and the Penitential Life of the Adult

We return to penance in the sense of self-denial and renunciation, but seen more as a requirement implicit in a life which is unceasingly under the influence of the adult's original conversion, and which finds its expression in the sacrament of penance. It is not possible to confuse this with those types of renunciation which spring from an embittered rejection of life and its goodness, or from the effort to dispel a vague psychological sense of guilt, or from masochism, or from Manichaeism.

What then are the truly Christian and adult motives for renunciation? We can analyze these briefly under three headings: (1) choice of the faith; (2) baptismal life; (3) apostolic life.

1. The decision of faith: A requirement for renunciation. It is easy to see that renunciation accompanies every stage of the decision of faith. To become believers, we must leave the world of arbitrary choice and fantasy to enter seriously into a life of true freedom. This presupposes choices in the direction of one's existence and in the search for happiness; it requires a sweeping away of unworthy goals and an effort at silence and recollection. Without some measure of self-denial, it is not possible to give up a shallow life, which finds its satisfaction at the level of the emotions and fixes the absolute values of life at each moment in the passing faces of beauty, pleasure, success, or vanity. Recall the Parable of the Sower: "And that which fell among the thorns, these are they who have heard [the Word which summons them to the faith], and as they go their way are choked by the cares and riches and pleasures of life" (Lk 8:14).

To become an adult believer in today's world requires a great deal of renunciation. We must not become caught in the coils of the many superficial attractions which beset us on every side. We must not allow ourselves to become immersed in material cares, in worldly planning, or in material comforts. We must not let ourselves be carried away by excessive optimism in the progress of science, or by breathtaking discoveries, or by the emotional build-up which so easily captivates people. We must rediscover the roots of freedom and the essential decisions which are in danger of being swallowed up in distractions. In particular, the young must learn to understand the merely passing value of the experiences which the world offers. They must not confuse the solid things of life with immediate impressions. They must learn to discover areas of silence, which permit them to withdraw from the maddening rhythms of daily life. All of this is at the opposite pole from a soft life of sentimentality and of reverie. It leaves no place for a life surrounded by every comfort. It is opposed to the dissipation of will power that inevitably results from a disorganized life.

In all this, the question is not simply one of self-mastery in the name of some human ideal: rather, the question concerns establishing a new center for one's existence, of harnessing one's liberty in order to face up to the challenge of Jesus Christ with a clear vision, and to respond to this challenge with courage and purposefulness. From the moment we decide to follow Christ, the words of the Lord are verified in us: "The Kingdom of Heaven has been enduring violent assault, and the violent have been seizing it by force" (Mt 11:12). One should aim at a detachment which seeks the good things in life according to their relative values, rather than a detachment which consists in a total rejection of all human pursuits. Speaking very practically, it is impossible to achieve a complete withdrawal from human experience. Moreover, such a futile effort brings with it the danger of arousing, in the long run, bitterness and regret that life has passed one by. Of course, this does not mean that one may commit sin in order to gain human experience.

2. *Baptismal life, a life of sacrifice.* Baptismal life is a continual process of conversion to Jesus Christ, spreading its influence into every corner of existence. Baptized into the death and resurrection of Jesus Christ the Christian should progress in this life under the direction of St. Paul's words: "Do you not know that we who have been baptized into Christ Jesus have been baptized into his death? For we were buried with him by means of baptism into death, in order that, just as Christ has arisen from the dead through the glory of the Father, so we also may walk in newness of life" (Rom 6:3-4). The demands of baptismal life, in the measure that this life becomes adult, can be summed up in the three following characteristics:

- It is a life that results from a decision. It develops the logical consequences of conversion to Jesus Christ, of the choice of the way of the Kingdom (thus rejecting the way of the world), and of obedience to the Holy Spirit. This development depends upon our intentions, convictions, and the direction which we give to life. The Fathers of the Church denounced as an attack on the very meaning of baptism the sin that they called dipsychia [two minds], which is a kind of hesitancy or split personality that is observable among some Christians.

- It is a life of sacrifice. It is a life offered to God. It is a life of obedience to his will, of sacrifice to his love and to the love of the brethren, in imitation of Jesus Christ as seen in his Paschal Mystery. This will never be the same thing as a successful life in the worldly sense of that term. "For no one lives to himself, and no one dies to himself. For if we live, we live to the Lord, or if we die, we die to the Lord. Therefore, whether we live or die, we are the Lord's. For to this end Christ died and rose again, that he might be Lord both of the dead and of the living" (Rom 14:7-10).

- It is a unified life. The whole person and his entire existence should progressively come under the influence of the power of Jesus Christ in his Pascal Mystery. Nothing is excluded, except sin itself. Jesus Christ becomes the motive of one's whole life and gives meaning, in terms of the Kingdom, to everything done by his baptized member. This is the teaching of St. Paul: "Whether you eat or drink, or do anything else, do all for the glory of God" (1 Cor 10:31).

It is evident that a baptismal life such as this requires effort and renunciation to collaborate with grace. Simplifying the matter a little, it is possible to discover three kinds of self-denial for the baptized adult without, however, wishing to indicate that these three types of asceticism correspond necessarily to the three requirements of baptismal life set forth above.

The first and fundamental asceticism consists in the effort of reflection and prayer that is necessary to discover the will of our Lord; the deliberate effort to eliminate arbitrary decisions and all superficiality from one's life; the effort to detach oneself in order to be able to renounce any value that is in competition with the faith, from the little tin gods that tend to draw one away from the one true God. This is the constant asceticism required by the decision of faith – to which is added the special challenge of perseverance.

Second, the Christian must practice a self-denial of atonement which results from the desire to make up for sin. Sin is always a divisive force, causing a division of loyalties, an effort to serve two masters at the same time. Whenever sin has sullied baptismal innocence, the Christian will strive to reaffirm more clearly his dedication to Christ alone by a complete break with his sinful past.

Finally, there is the self-denial of purification by which the purity of one's Christian motives is put to the test and by which the influence of faith in one's life is intensified. Christ spoke of this purifying self-denial and compared it with the action of the· vinedresser who cuts and prunes the vines so that they may bear even more fruit (see Jn 15). Only by accepting certain trials can baptized Christians be sure, existentially, that they live and act only for Jesus Christ, or, at least, that they are making progress toward unity of life in Christ. "Unless the grain of wheat fall into the ground and die, it remains alone. But if it dies, it brings forth much fruit" (Jn 12:24).

Does not everything consist in understanding that baptismal life, life sacrificed with Jesus Christ, is truly a higher kind of life, and that sacrifice has meaning only because of the life which God gives and because of the fruit which God wishes to cultivate there? This is a discovery that can be made only in maturity.

3. *The apostolic life is a life of self-sacrifice.* Under this heading we shall group everything that expresses baptismal life in the world under the forms of fraternal charity and of bearing witness. Thus, it will become evident that new motives for Christian self-denial are implied in the apostolic life.

Once we have accepted the idea that nothing belongs to us except what has been loaned to us for the service of others, we may be sure that we will often have to go against our own tastes and that we will have to forego our immediate needs, even the most legitimate. We must be prepared to endure sickness and to give up a measure of the care of ourselves. This detachment and mastery of self takes on the character of a gift and of a kind of service to others in the cause of Jesus Christ. Still more is required of the adult believer who enters into the mystery of the apostolate.

What else is martyrdom but witness culminating in the gift of life itself? Every witness to Christ must necessarily know this even though he may not have to go so far as to sacrifice his physical life. Jesus Christ has foretold that his witnesses would be a sign of contradiction and the object of persecutions, because the disciple is not above the master. Even though he may not be a martyr, the apostle of Jesus Christ will be called upon much more than the servant of any human ideal to sacrifice his personal preferences, time, interest, good name, and rest, all for the sake of the work of the Kingdom. We must read again those impassioned words of St. Paul to the Corinthians: "In labor and hardships, in many sleepless nights, in hunger and thirst, in fasting often, in cold and nakedness. Besides those outer things, there is my daily pressing anxiety, the care of all the churches!" (2 Cor 11:27-28.)

He is not speaking of a pleasure trip, but of a crusade. Moreover, for the Apostle, every renunciation accepted out of love and concern for the Kingdom is of benefit to the Church: "I rejoice now in the sufferings I bear for your sake; and what is lacking of the sufferings of Christ I fill up in my flesh for his body, which is the Church" (Col 1:24). Once again, the Christian endures trials and practices renunciation in order to spread the life of Christ. "Always bearing in our body the dying of Jesus, so that the life of Jesus may be made manifest in our bodily frame" (2 Cor 4:10).

Preparing Adults for the Self-denial of the Gospels

An indispensable psychological presupposition for maturity is an adult relationship to reality, with its consequent balanced judgments, and the wisdom to thank God for having clearly understood human experience in a way that is not possible to the pagan mentality. There is another equally indispensable presupposition which is spiritual. It consists in a relation of all one's existence to the mysteries of Christ, involving a life of sacrifice with Christ, a life of unceasing conversion of heart. Presupposing these two conditions, the following should be observed regarding the practice of penance:

1) In our efforts to form the Christian mentality of renunciation, we must take care always to supply Christian motives for the

actions that are suggested or demanded and to show their significance in relation to the sacrifice of the Mass. Faith and the Mass can give a positive meaning to many ordinary attitudes and actions which otherwise would never rise above the level of simple ethical conduct. A Christian life without self-denial is an idle dream, and a self-denial unrelated to faith and the Mass is nothing more than moralism.

2) We must also strive to make sure that renunciation does not remain a kind of external conformism. By an act of free will, we incorporate these renunciations into a life of penance; we are far from being content with any purely external exercise. These practices should liberate our heart so as to leave us free to become slaves of Christ and of our brothers and sisters and of the Kingdom. We should communicate a sense of personal adaptation, rather than simply submitting to a list of ascetical practices to be performed. This will permit us to be strict without rigorism and without pettiness.

3) We should not neglect to convey the fact that Christian detachment is not without joy. God loves the cheerful giver and he brings this joy to a perfection that only he can impart. Such was the joy of St. Francis of Assisi, composing the canticle of Creation immediately after he had received the marks of the passion of Christ in his flesh. This happened as his life drew to its close, when he was worn out in the service of Christ and of his brethren, when he was blind, and when his brothers had turned him out. Such is the joy of the Gospels, a joy very far from that of this world. It is the joy promised to the believer who gives himself without reserve to the demands of his Christian maturity. "These things I have spoken to you that my joy may be in you, and that your joy may be made full" (Jn 15:11).

Scripture Index

Prv		Rom	
1:22	• 30	6:3-4	• 93
Jer		7:15-20	• xi
35:15	• 80	14:7-10	• 94
Mt		1 Cor	
6:21	• 34	10:31	• 94
11:12	• 93	13:11	• 29
12:41	• 80	13:	• 55
18:3	• 29	14:20	• 29
23:8-13	• 72	2 Cor	
Mk		3:6	• 70
1:14-15	• 78	4:10	• 97
1:15	• 35	11:27-28	• 96
Lk		Gal	
Jn		5:6	• 49
2:52	• 27	5:16	• 25, 70
3:8	• 80	Eph	
5:32	• 81	3:17	• 34
8:14	• 92	4:13	• xi, 31
12:24	• 95	5:8-11	• 88
15:	• 95	5:17	• 71
15:17	• 90	Phil	
15:18	• 81	2:5-12	• 69
15:11	• 98	Col	
17:3	• 38	1:24	• 97
22:24-28	• 72	1 Pt	
22:7-11	• 72	5:2-3	• 72
Acts		1 Jn	
11:18	• 83	3:5-10	• 87
17:30-31	• 81	3:6	• 81
2:38	• 80	Rev	
5:29	• 75	2:4-5	• 81

PIERRE-ANDRE LIEGE, O.P.

www.ingramcontent.com/pod-product-compliance
Lightning Source LLC
Chambersburg PA
CBHW060846050426
42453CB00008B/861